Great Patchwork: Working with Squares and Rectangles

Great Patchwork:
Working with
Squares and Rectangles

BETTER HOMES AND GARDENS® BOOKS

DES MOINES, IOWA

Better Homes and Gardens® Books, an imprint of Meredith® Books:
President, Book Group: Joseph J. Ward
Vice President, Editorial Director: Elizabeth P. Rice

Executive Editor: Maryanne Bannon
Senior Editor: Carol Spier
Assistant Editor: Bonita Eckhaus
Selections Editor: Eleanor Levie
Technical Editor: Cyndi Marsico
Technical Assistant: Diane Rode Schneck
Copy Editor: Melanie Hulse
Book Design: Beth Tondreau Design/M. Leo Albert, Daniel Rutter
Technical Artist: Phoebe Adams Gaughan
Photographer: Steven Mays
Photo Stylist: Susan Piatt
Production Manager: Bill Rose

The editors would like to thank Barley Sheaf Farm Inn, Holicong, Pennsylvania, for
sharing their premises for photography. Thanks also to Laura Fisher Antiques, New York City;
Gypsy's Antique Quilts, Davidson, North Carolina; and Menagerie of River Oaks, Houston,
Texas, for their kind assistance in the search for quilts to include in this volume.

ISBN: 0-696-20021-X
Library of Congress Catalog Card Number: 94-075284

Printed in the United States of America
10 9 8 7 6 5 4 3 2 1

All of us at Better Homes and Gardens® Books are dedicated to offering you,
our customer, the best books we can create. We are particularly concerned that
all of our instructions for making projects are clear and accurate.
Please address your correspondence to Customer Service, Meredith® Press,
150 East 52nd Street, New York, NY 10022.

If you would like to order additional copies of any of our books,
call 1-800-678-2803 or check with your local bookstore.

Contents

Squares and rectangles—*clear and regular*—*patchwork of timeless appeal. Here, we invite you to choose among patterns that are comfortable and familiar, like Coverlet; or filled with unexpected proportions, like Prism Patches; or at once simple and complex, like the color-dependent one-patch pieces hanging in our Watercolor Gallery. Many of these quilts could not be easier—though for some you must keep your wits in order. Looking for a challenge? Chevron will test patience and skill, while the* **CHANGING COLORS** *and* **CHANGING SETS** *features suggest wonderful variations to develop for each quilt.*

These symbols, found on the opening page of each project, identify suggested levels of experience needed to make the projects in this book. However, you will see within these pages many interpretations of each project, and the editors hope you will find for each something easily achievable or challenging, as you wish.

 New Quilter   *Confident Quilter*   *Expert Quilter*

Prism Patches

BY MIMI SHIMMIN
PIECED AND QUILTED BY
CAROLINE KEARNEY

It is not true that there is nothing new under the sun. Although squares and rectangles are the units with which so many classic and beloved quilt patterns are composed, we were determined to put them together in an original manner. Mimi Shimmin created an uneven 9-patch and set it spinning. The throw pillows recombine the units in various ways. Compare Mimi's block with the Coverlet block, page 22—perhaps what goes around, comes around, after all.

Note: All dimensions except for binding are finished size. We have selected a representative color to depict the 13 bright solids on this quilt. Refer to the photographs, opposite and on page 15, to see the actual colors and their distribution.

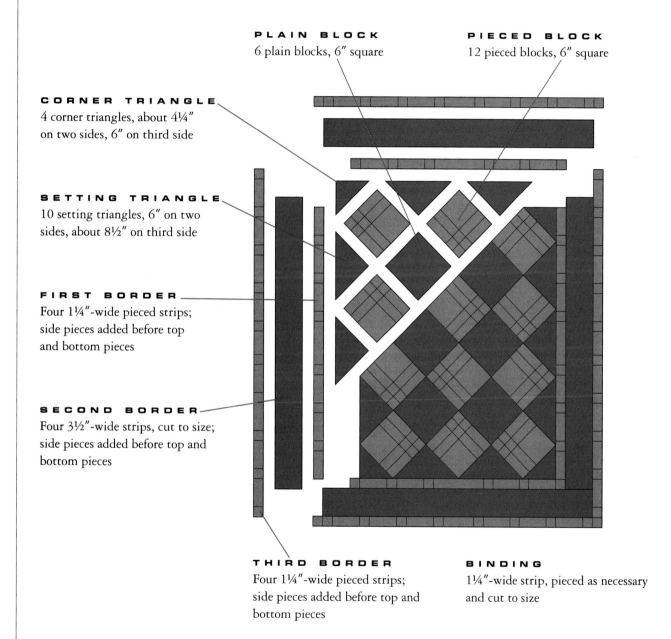

PLAIN BLOCK
6 plain blocks, 6″ square

PIECED BLOCK
12 pieced blocks, 6″ square

CORNER TRIANGLE
4 corner triangles, about 4¼″ on two sides, 6″ on third side

SETTING TRIANGLE
10 setting triangles, 6″ on two sides, about 8½″ on third side

FIRST BORDER
Four 1¼″-wide pieced strips; side pieces added before top and bottom pieces

SECOND BORDER
Four 3½″-wide strips, cut to size; side pieces added before top and bottom pieces

THIRD BORDER
Four 1¼″-wide pieced strips; side pieces added before top and bottom pieces

BINDING
1¼″-wide strip, pieced as necessary and cut to size

Yardages are based on 44" fabric. Prepare templates, if desired, referring to drafting schematics. Cut strips and patches following cutting schematics and chart; see *Using the Cutting Charts*, page 92. Cut binding as directed below. Except for drafting schematics, which give finished sizes, all dimensions include ¼" seam allowance and strips include extra length, unless otherwise stated. (NOTE: Angles on all patches are either 45° or 90°.)

DIMENSIONS

FINISHED PLAIN BLOCK
6" square; about 8½" diagonal

FINISHED PIECED BLOCK
6" square; about 8½" diagonal

FINISHED QUILT
About 37½" × 46"

GREAT BINDING TIP

If you want to make bias binding, you will need an additional ¼ yd. of black solid. Cut strips on a 45° diagonal and piece as needed.

MATERIALS

ASSORTED SOLIDS
¼ yd. each of 13 different bright solids, chosen from among shades of yellow, orange, red, blue, green, purple, and tan; see the *Great Planning Tip*, page 10.

BLACK SOLID
1¾ yds.

BINDING
Use ¼ yd. black solid, cut and pieced, to make a 1¼" × 180" straight-grain strip.

BACKING *
3 yds.

BATTING *

THREAD

*Backing and batting should be cut and pieced as necessary so they are at least 4" larger than quilt on all sides, then trimmed to size after quilting.

DRAFTING SCHEMATICS

(No seam allowance added)

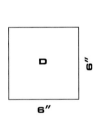

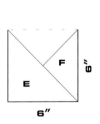

CUTTING SCHEMATICS

(Seam allowance included)

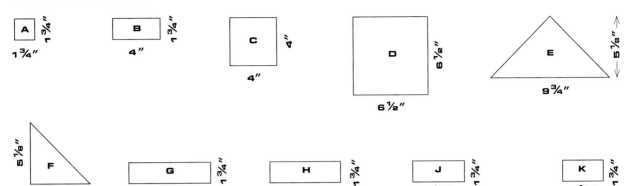

		FIRST CUT		SECOND CUT			
				Number of Pieces			
Fabric and Yardage	**Number of Pieces**	**Size**	For Quilt Center	For First Border	For Third Border	**Shape**	
PATCHES							
Assorted Solids ¼ yd. each	13	1¾″ × 20″	48	24	40	A[1]	
	13	1¾″ × 40″	48	20	28	B[2]	
	—	—	12	—	—	C[3]	
	1	1¾″ × 20″	—	2	—	G[4]	
	1	1¾″ × 20″	—	2	—	H[4]	
	1	1¾″ × 10″	—	—	2	J[4]	
	1	1¾″ × 10″	—	—	2	K[4]	
Black Solid [5] 1½ yds.	1	6½″ × 40″	6	—	—	D	
	2	5⅛″ × 40″	10	—	—	E	
	1	5⅛″ × 40″	4	—	—	F	
SECOND BORDER							
	2	4″ × 45″					
	2	4″ × 47″					

[1] Cut one strip from each of 13 different solids. Cut 8 or 9 A's from each strip to total 112.
[2] Cut one strip from each of 13 different solids. Cut 7 or 8 B's from each strip to total 96.
[3] Cut one C from each of 12 different solids.
[4] Cut G's, H's, J's and K's from 8 different solids.
[5] Cut all strips on lengthwise grain.

GREAT PLANNING TIP

The placement of bright solids on this quilt may appear at first glance to be totally random, but a closer look reveals the careful planning that went into creating that effect; see the photographs on pages 6 and 15 for the actual placement and distribution of colors.

Mimi Shimmin used a total of 13 different bright solids on her quilt, but the design could work as easily with 12 (the number of pieced blocks in the quilt center). If you study the design, you will notice that each of the pieced blocks is made of 9 patches cut from 9 different colors, and each of the large squares in these blocks is a different color. The center patches on the four sides of both pieced borders were cut from 8 different colors, as were the 8 corner squares. Even the trios of small squares in the corners of the outer pieced border were cut from 12 different colors. In general, no two patches of the same bright solid touch on any side or corner. Notice also that the orientation of individual pieced blocks is not repeated in any horizontal or vertical row they form.

Use the diagram on page 17 to plan your quilt. After all of your patches have been cut out, lay them out to be sure you are satisfied with the arrangement of the bright colors before doing any stitching.

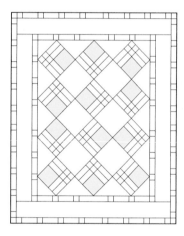

LARGE SQUARES

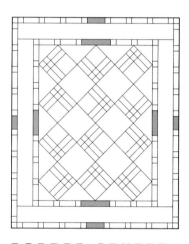

BORDER CENTER
PATCHES

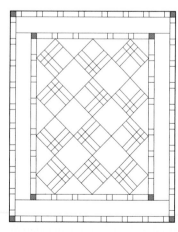

CORNER SQUARES

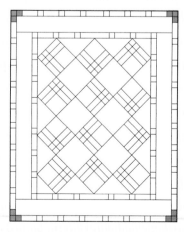

CORNER TRIOS

Note: Directions are given below for making one pieced block; see the **Great Planning Tip,** *opposite. Amounts for making all 12 pieced blocks at the same time are given in parentheses.*

Pieced Block

1. Join 4 A's to make one (12) 4-patch.

2. Join 4 (98) B's in pairs.

3. Arrange units as shown. Join units to make 2 rows. Join rows.

FINISHED PIECED BLOCK

Quilt Center

Arrange units as shown. Join units to make rows. Join rows.

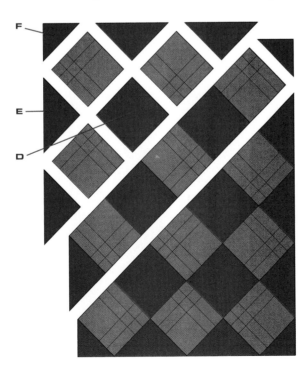

Borders

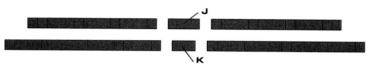

1. Assemble pieced first border; see also the *Great Pieced Border Tip*, below.

- Join A's and B's as shown to make 4 short strips and 4 long strips.
- Stitch G's between pairs of short strips and H's between pairs of long strips.

- Join border to quilt center, first long strips at sides, then short strips at top and bottom.

2. Join plain second border to quilt, first long strips at sides, then short strips at top and bottom.

3. Assemble pieced third border.

- Join A's and B's as shown to make 4 short strips and 4 long strips.
- Stitch J's between pairs of short strips and K's between pairs of long strips.

- Join border to quilt, first long strips at sides, then short strips at top and bottom.

GREAT PIECED BORDER TIP

You can ensure that your pieced borders will fit your quilt exactly by adjusting the center patches G, H, J and K.

Cut the center patches about 3″ longer than indicated on the cutting schematics, page 9. Assemble the ends of each border strip, then trim its center patch so that when it is stitched between the strip ends the resulting border strip will be the same length as the quilt edge to which it will be joined.

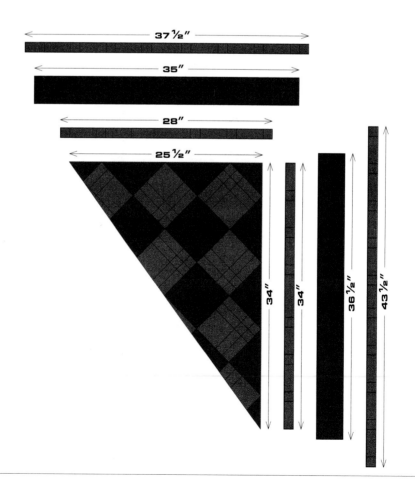

Finishing

1. Mark quilting designs on quilt top.

◆ *For quilt center:* Mark motifs on plain blocks and setting triangles only, placing lines 1″ and 2″ from seams. Mark a line on each corner triangle between long edge and opposite corner.

◆ *For second border:* Mark on-point squares, centered between long seams: Mark a 1¾″ square in each corner, ½″ from seams, then mark seven 1½″ squares on each half of top and bottom border strips, working from large corner squares in toward center; mark center square, sized as necessary to fit. Mark border sides in same manner, making nine 1½″ squares on each side of center.

2. Prepare batting and backing.

3. Assemble quilt layers.

4. Quilt in-the-ditch on all seams of pieced blocks and on inner and outer edges of pieced borders. Quilt on all marked lines.

5. Trim batting and backing to ⅜″ beyond outermost seam line.

6. Bind quilt edges.

GREAT SIZING IDEA

If you double the size of the wall-hanging components (enlarge them to 200%), they will be just the right size to make a 75″ × 92″ twin coverlet. To enlarge the quilt to 94″ × 111″ for full/queen, add four more borders to the twin coverlet, continuing the pattern of alternating plain and pieced borders.

For the twin, you will need about four times as much fabric as for the wallhanging. For the full/queen, you will need four times the fabric as for the wallhanging, plus an extra 3 yds. of black solid to make the additional plain borders.

TWIN
3 borders

FULL/QUEEN
7 borders

The components that make up the Prism Patches wallhanging can be recombined to create many different designs. All of the pillows shown below can easily be made from fabric left over from the wallhanging. Try making one or more of our pillows or design your own. Use any or all of the components from the wallhanging and add any new elements as necessary.

Pillow #1 (15½" square finished size) is made of 9 black C's framed with sashing composed of assorted color A's and B's. Pillow #2 (also 15½" square) is made of one assorted color pieced block, 4 black C's, 4 new black rectangles, sashing made of assorted color A's, B's, and 4 new color rectangles. Pillow #3 (12" square) has no black units at all and is made of 4 assorted color pieced blocks.

Follow the cutting chart for the number of patches to cut for each pillow, or cut your patches based on a graph paper pattern of your own design.

Piece together the pillow top, then assemble the layers and quilt in-the-ditch on all seams or as desired. Add a pillow back and corded piping, and stuff firmly with fiberfill; for the larger pillows, you can insert a 16"-square knife-edge pillow form instead.

PILLOW		
Fabric and Yardage	Number of Pieces	Size/Shape
FOR PILLOW #1 (BLACK BLOCKS WITH SASHING)		
Assorted Solids	16	A
	24	B
Black Solid	9	C
FOR PILLOW #2 (BLACK AND ASSORTED COLOR BLOCKS WITH SASHING)		
Assorted Solids	8	A
	12	B
	4	2" × 6½"
Black Solid	4	C
	4	4" × 6½"
FOR PILLOW #3 (ASSORTED COLOR BLOCKS)		
Assorted Solids	16	A
	16	B
	4	C

Y ou can have a lot of fun planning colors for this quilt, which can spin from child-like to sophisticated with your palette. To give it a quiet look, use only cool colors, or nine or more values of any one color. To give it a classic air, use no more than three colors. Try repeating the background color in the innermost small square patch.

Photocopy this page, then create your own color scheme using colored pencils or markers. Refer to the examples shown, or design a unique arrangement to match your decor or please your fancy. See what happens when adjacent corners of the pieced blocks are the same color.

If you turn all of the pieced blocks in one direction, this pattern will be less exuberant. Omitting the plain blocks will create interesting allover patterns. Note how different a simple straight set variation appears to your eye, and how sashing changes the balance. Redistribute your colors to enhance any of these variations.

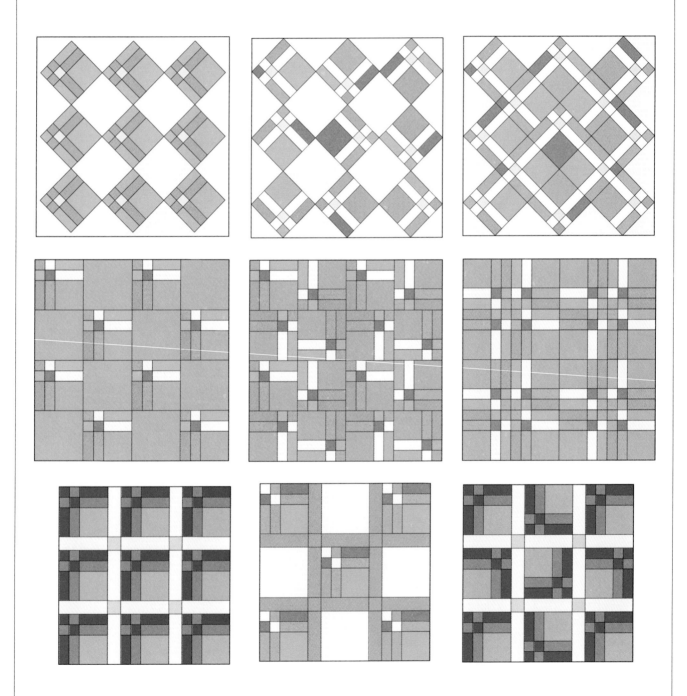

Honor to the 9-Patch

Perhaps because it combines simplicity with a sometimes surprising versatility, the basic 9-patch pattern—nine identical squares arranged in a 3 x 3 grid—is an enduring favorite. Many a beginning quilter's first project has been a simple two-tone 9-patch quilt, and sophisticated designers continue to find fresh and unexpected ways to use this well-loved block. Indeed, many of the blocks in this book can be seen as variations on the basic 9-patch.

The nine sections of the block can be resized to include both squares and rectangles, and any or all of these can be subdivided into 3-, 4-, or 9-patches, or myriad other patterns—but as long as the characteristic configuration of two horizontal and two vertical seams forming a grid remains, the block is still a 9-patch and can be assembled as such.

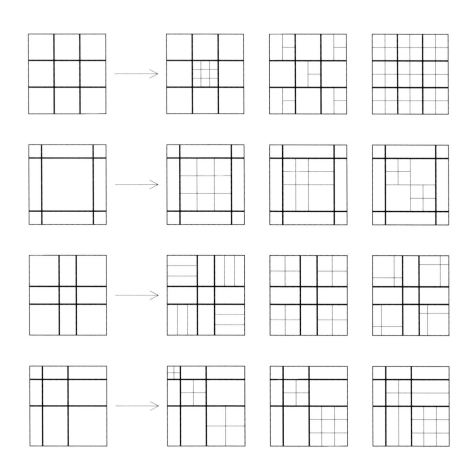

The placement and balance of color can change the look of a 9-patch block, defining a regular two-tone checkerboard or creating a dynamic multicolor arrangement whose complete pattern appears only after several blocks have been joined. Look at other Changing Colors pages in this book to see the effect of positive/negative block arrangement and of plain alternate blocks with different 9-patch colorations.

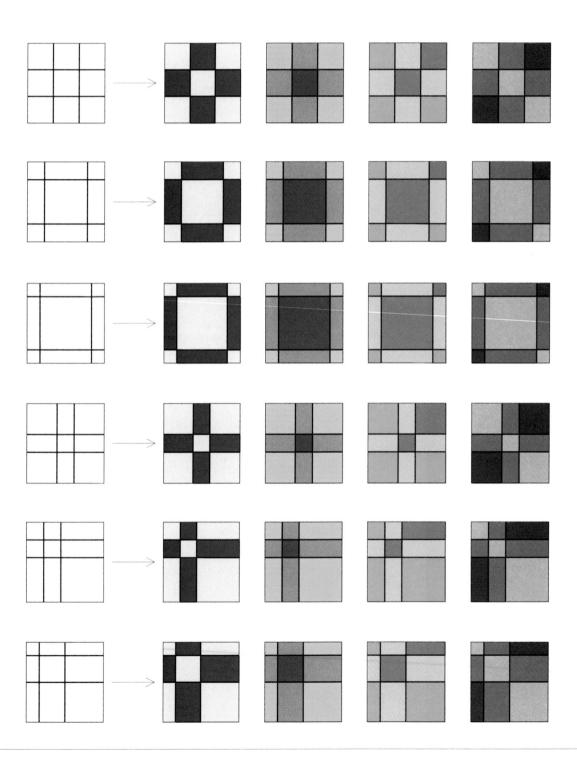

It's hard to go wrong setting 9-patch blocks. Whether you alternate them with plain blocks, repeat them one against another, set them squarely or on point, you will have a pleasing quilt. Depending upon the block variation with which you are working, a simple set may be all you need to create an apparently complex pattern. Consider as well developing an irregular repetition of blocks to create a larger overall pattern.

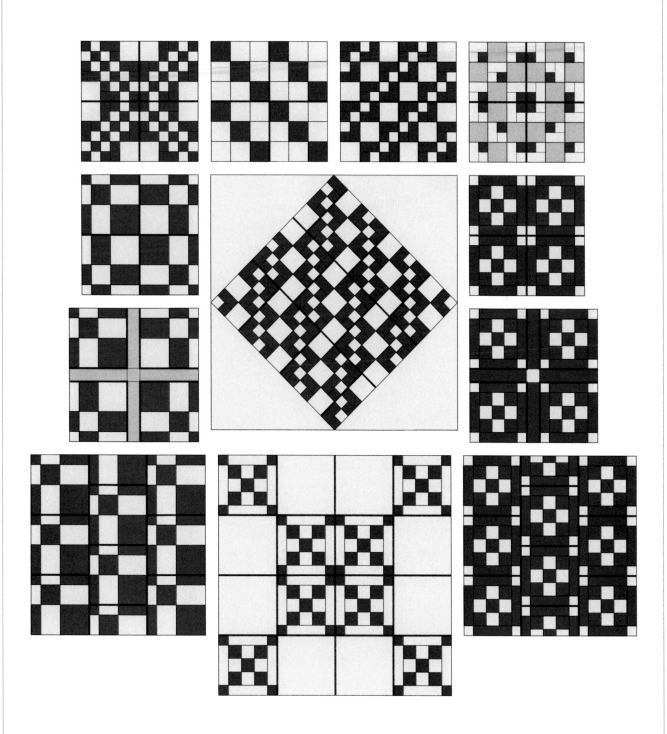

Coverlet

One simple block in a positive/negative repeat gives this charming old quilt the look of an overshot woven coverlet. We will never know whether the quiltmaker used three different ginghams by choice or necessity, but whatever her reason, their random placement adds to the comfortable, homey effect of the patchwork. To make a very contemporary version of this quilt, use more colors to emphasize the zigzag diagonal in the overall pattern; see CHANGING COLORS on page 30.

Note: All dimensions are finished size. This quilt is a nonstandard size. It may be big enough for a double bed if you turn it sideways—use the length of the quilt across the width of the bed. Amounts for full/queen are given in parentheses.

NEGATIVE BLOCK
28 (36) negative blocks, 10½" square

POSITIVE BLOCK
28 (36) positive blocks, 10½" square

BORDER
Four 3"-wide border strips, cut to size; side pieces added before top and bottom pieces

BINDING
Self-binding

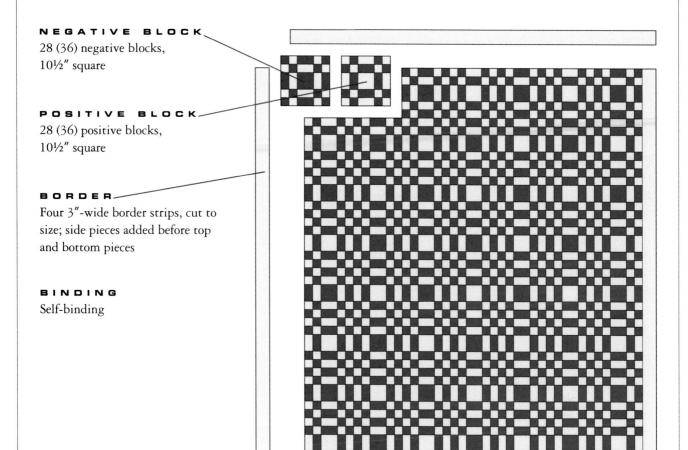

Yardages are based on 44″ fabric. Prepare templates, if desired, referring to drafting schematics. Cut strips and patches following cutting schematics and charts; see *Using the Cutting Charts*, page 92; see also the *Great Piecing Tip*, page 26, for an alternate method of cutting and piecing. Except for drafting schematics, which give finished sizes, all dimensions include ¼″ seam allowance and strips include extra length, unless otherwise stated. (NOTE: Angles on all patches are 90°.)

DIMENSIONS

FINISHED BLOCK
10½″ square;
about 14¾″ diagonal

FINISHED QUILT
79½″ × 90″ (90″ × 100½″)

MATERIALS

☐ ECRU SOLID
7¼ (8¾) yds.; see the *Great Fabric Saving Tip*, below.

■ NAVY/WHITE CHECK
4½ (5¾) yds.

SELF-BINDING
No extra fabric or cutting required.

BACKING *
8 (9) yds.; see also the *Great Fabric Saving Tip*, below.

BATTING *

THREAD

*Backing and batting should be cut and pieced as necessary so they are at least 4″ larger than quilt on all sides, then trimmed to size after quilting.

DRAFTING SCHEMATICS
(No seam allowance added)

CUTTING SCHEMATICS
(Seam allowance included)

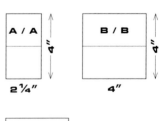

FIRST CUT				SECOND CUT		
				Number of Pieces		
Fabric and Yardage	Number of Pieces	Size	Method	For 28 (36) Positive Blocks	For 28 (36) Negative Blocks	Shape
STRIP-PIECED PATCHES*						
Ecru Solid and Navy/White Check 4 (5) yds. each	29 (36)	2¼″ × 40″		224 (288)	224 (288)	A/A
	29 (36)	2¼″ × 40″				
	23 (29)	2¼″ × 40″		112 (144)	112 (144)	B/B
	23 (29)	2¼″ × 40″				
* Join strips lengthwise as shown.						

FIRST CUT			SECOND CUT		
			Number of Pieces		
Fabric and Yardage	Number of Pieces	Size	For 28 (36) Positive Blocks	For 28 (36) Negative Blocks	Shape
PLAIN PATCHES					
Ecru Solid ½ (¾) yd.	3 (4)	4″ × 40″	28 (36)	—	C
Navy/White Check ½ (¾) yd.	3 (4)	4″ × 40″	—	28 (36)	C

Fabric and Yardage	Number of Pieces	Size
BORDER*		
Ecru Solid 2¾ (3) yds.	2	3½″ × 86″ (3½″ × 96″)
	2	3½″ × 90″ (3½″ × 101″)
* See the *Great Fabric Saving Tip*, opposite.		

GREAT PIECING TIP

You may find it quicker to make the blocks for Coverlet by strip-piecing block units as shown below instead of cutting and joining smaller pieced and plain 9-patch units. Only two different pieced bands are needed to cut the four units that make up both the positive and negative blocks.

POSITIVE BAND

NEGATIVE BAND

1. From ecru solid cut 40 (52) strips, 2¼" × 40", and 10 (13) strips, 4" × 40". Cut an equal number of strips from navy/white check.

2. Join strips as shown to make 10 (13) positive bands and 10 (13) negative bands.

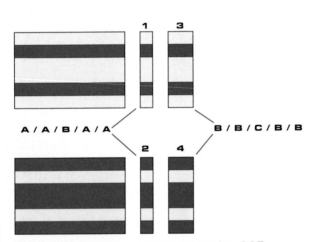

A / A / B / A / A   B / B / C / B / B

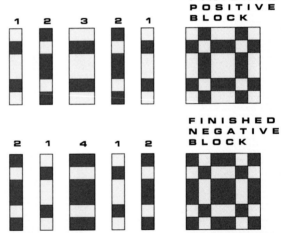

FINISHED POSITIVE BLOCK

FINISHED NEGATIVE BLOCK

3. Cut bands into strips to make 112 (144) each of 2¼"-wide units #1 and #2. Cut 28 (36) each of 4"-wide units #3 and #4.

4. Join units as shown to make 28 (36) positive blocks and 28 (36) negative blocks.

The size of this quilt can be adjusted easily from twin to full/queen by increasing the number of blocks to make one additional row and one additional column. Refer to the cutting charts, page 25, for the number of pieces to cut for the different sizes.

TWIN
56 blocks in a 7 × 8 layout

FULL/QUEEN
72 blocks in an 8 × 9 layout

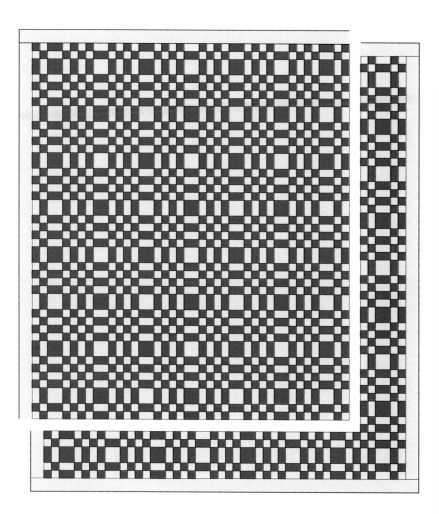

GREAT SIZING TIP

Because this pattern will repeat continuously no matter how many blocks are placed in each row or column, you can plan your quilt to be almost any size you wish. Just remember that the length of each edge will be a multiple of 10½" (one block) plus 6" (the width of a pair of border strips).

4 blocks in a 2 × 2 layout = 27"-square wallhanging

9 blocks in a 3 × 3 layout = 37½"-square wallhanging

15 blocks in a 3 × 5 layout = 37½" × 58½" crib quilt

Positive and Negative Blocks

Directions are given below for making one positive block; see also the *Great Piecing Tip*, page 26. Amounts for making all 28 (twin) or 36 (full/queen) positive blocks at the same time are given in parentheses. Rotate the pieced units and join them to dark C's to make the same number of negative blocks.

1. Sew A/A's together in pairs, alternating colors, to make 4 (112) (144) four-patches.

2. Arrange units as shown. Join units to make 3 rows. Join rows.

FINISHED POSITIVE BLOCK

FINISHED NEGATIVE BLOCK

Quilt Center

Arrange blocks as shown, alternating positive and negative blocks. Join blocks to make rows. Join rows.

TWIN

FULL/QUEEN

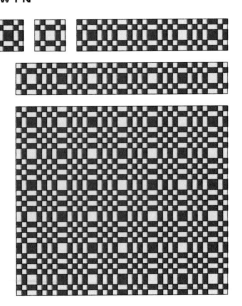

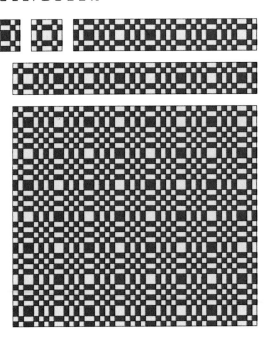

Border

Join border to quilt center, first long strips at sides, then short strips at top and bottom.

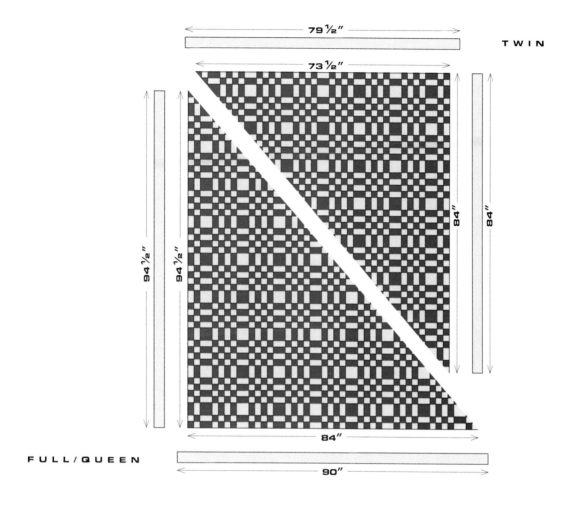

TWIN

FULL/QUEEN

79½"

73½"

94½"

94½"

84"

84"

84"

90"

Finishing

1. Mark quilting designs on quilt top.
- *For quilt center:* Mark an allover on-point square grid, using corners of patches as a guide.
- *For border:* Mark lines ¼" and 1½" from inner border seam all around.

2. Prepare batting and backing.

3. Assemble quilt layers.

4. Quilt on all marked lines.

5. Trim backing even with quilt top. Trim batting ¼" smaller than fabric layers.

6. For self-binding, press fabric edges ¼" to inside. Slipstitch quilt top and backing together along folds.

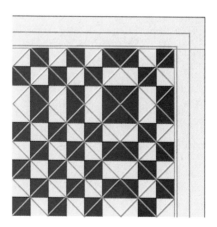

This pattern is at once familiar and unusual, and your use of color can turn it from classic to contemporary. It holds all sorts of secondary patterns that emerge with careful placement of contrasting color—have fun, but keep in mind that as the simple blocks become more complex, our directions may need some modification.

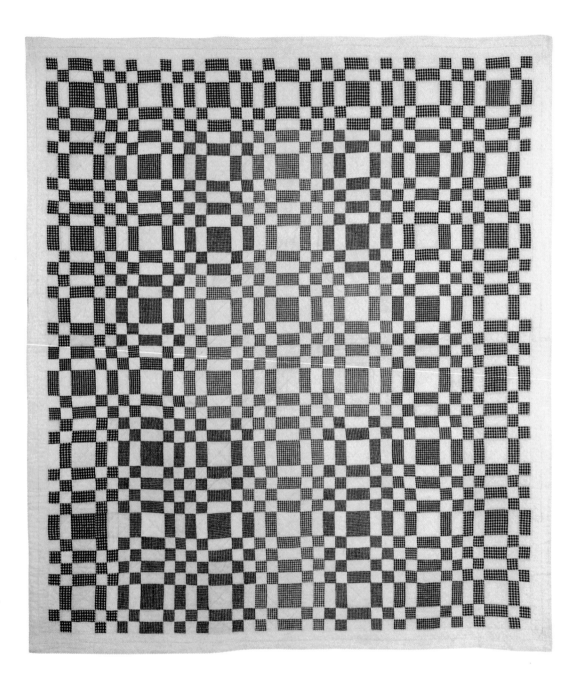

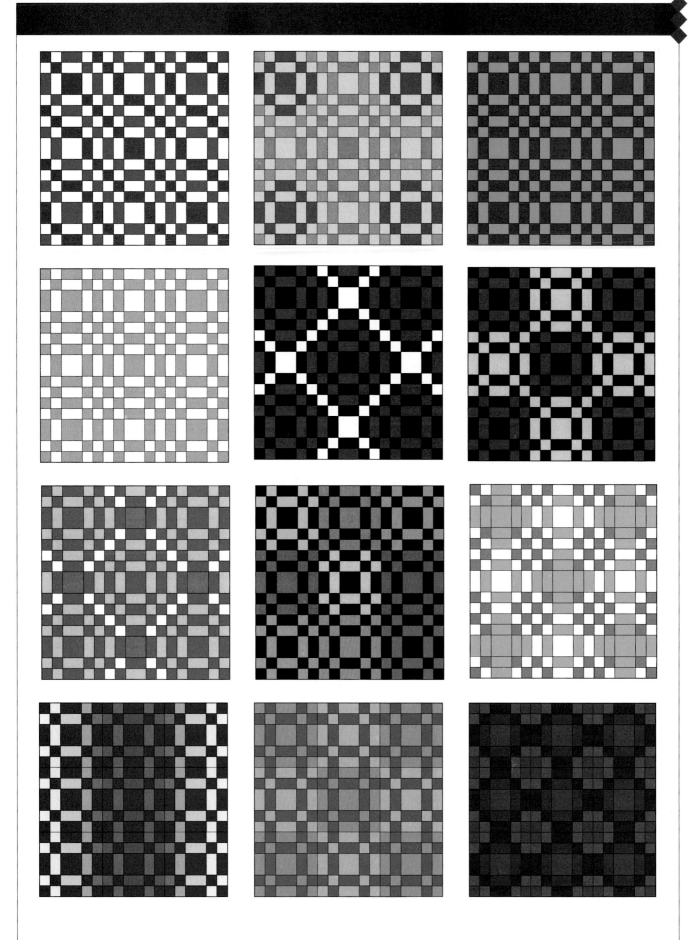

Photocopy this page, then create your own color scheme using colored pencils or markers. Refer to the examples shown, or create one that is completely original. You can even weave ribbons through a dark ground—replace all the white areas shown in the photos with horizontal or vertical bands of bright color.

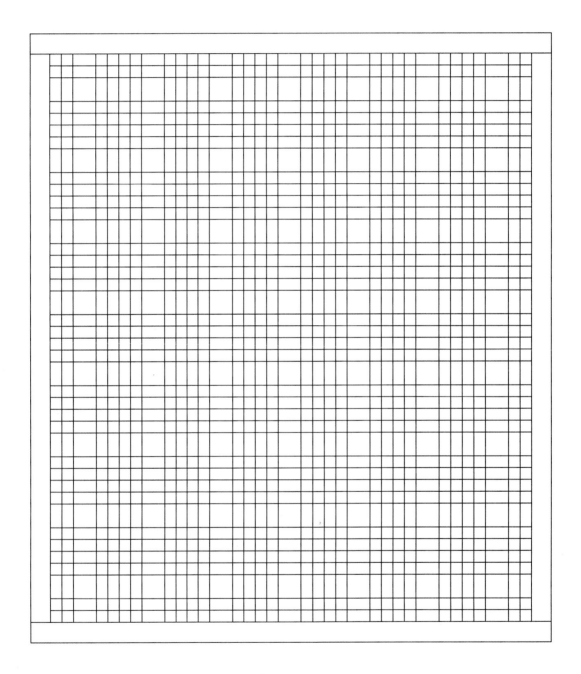

Any simple repeat of the Coverlet block, like the positive/negative set shown in the photographs, will create a pattern that is full of motion. Try a straight or diagonal set with all positive (or all negative) blocks, or an offset repeat (use partial blocks to complete the pattern). Use sashing or plain setting blocks for a more sedate effect.

Puss in the Corner

The elegance and simplicity of this pattern assure that it will never be out of vogue. Signed on the back by Cornelia Palmer, this exquisite chintz and muslin example dates from 1830. Palmer must be admired not only for her lovely quilting and wonderful use of fabric, but also for her thrift and patience —many of the square and triangular patches are themselves pieced from small, and not always matching, bits of cloth. On the trunk, in a diagonally set version of the pattern, the 9-patch blocks alternate with contrasting plain blocks.

Note: All dimensions except for binding are finished size. This quilt is a nonstandard size.
You might prefer to use the length of the quilt across the width of your bed. Amounts
below are for full/queen. Differing amounts for twin are given in parentheses.
We have selected a representative color to depict the assorted prints of the quilt center.
Make about 13 (11) block centers each from mustard, blue, green, and brown prints to get a good
mix. Refer to the photographs, opposite and on page 42, to see the actual distribution of colors.

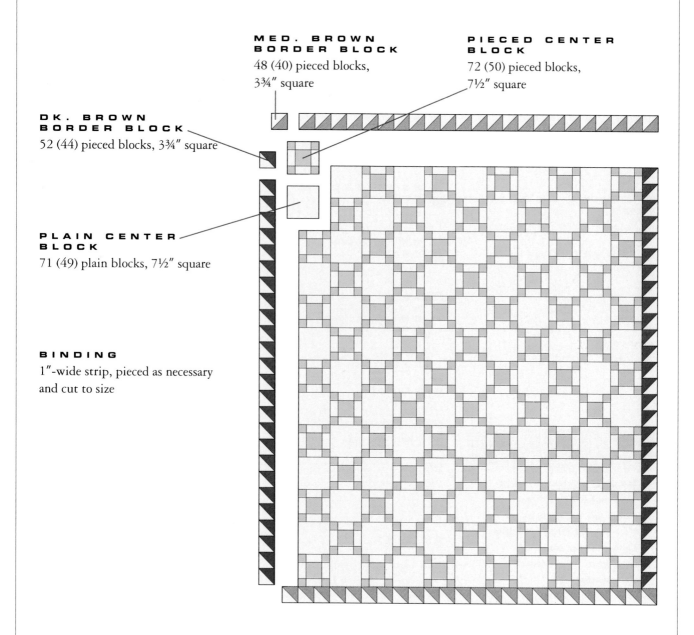

MED. BROWN BORDER BLOCK
48 (40) pieced blocks, 3¾" square

PIECED CENTER BLOCK
72 (50) pieced blocks, 7½" square

DK. BROWN BORDER BLOCK
52 (44) pieced blocks, 3¾" square

PLAIN CENTER BLOCK
71 (49) plain blocks, 7½" square

BINDING
1"-wide strip, pieced as necessary and cut to size

Note: Sizes and amounts below are for full/queen.
Differing sizes and amounts for twin are given in parentheses.

Yardages are based on 44" fabric. Prepare templates, if desired, referring to drafting schematics. Cut strips and patches following cutting schematics and charts; see *Using the Cutting Charts*, page 92. Cut binding as directed below. Except for drafting schematics, which give finished sizes, all dimensions include ¼" seam allowance and strips include extra length, unless otherwise stated. (NOTE: Angles on all patches are either 45° or 90°.)

DIMENSIONS

FINISHED CENTER BLOCK
7½" square; about 10⅝" diagonal

FINISHED BORDER BLOCK
3¾" square; about 5¼" diagonal

FINISHED QUILT
90" × 105" (75" × 90")

GREAT BINDING TIP

If you want to make bias binding, you will need an additional ½ (¼) yd. of muslin solid. Cut strips on a 45° diagonal and piece as needed.

MATERIALS

☐ **MUSLIN SOLID**
8¼ (6½) yds.

▨ **MED. BROWN PRINT**
¾ yd.

■ **DK. BROWN PRINT**
¾ yd.

▨ **ASSORTED MUSTARD, BLUE, GREEN, AND BROWN PRINTS**
3 (2¾) yds. equally divided among at least 4 different colors

BINDING
Use ½ yd. muslin solid, cut and pieced, to make a 1" × 400" (1" × 340") straight-grain strip.

BACKING *
9¾ (8½) yds.

BATTING *

THREAD

*Backing and batting should be cut and pieced as necessary so they are at least 4" larger than quilt on all sides, then trimmed to size after quilting.

DRAFTING SCHEMATICS
(No seam allowance added)

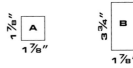

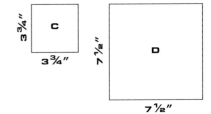

CUTTING
SCHEMATICS

(Seam allowance included)

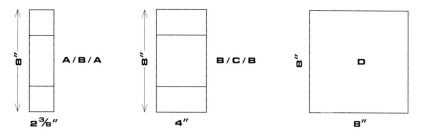

FIRST CUT			SECOND CUT		
Fabric and Yardage	Number of Pieces	Size	Method	Number of Pieces	Shape
STRIP-PIECED PATCHES[1]					
Muslin Solid and Assorted Prints[2] 1½ yds. each	18 (14)	2⅜" × 40"		144 (100)	A/B/A
	9 (7)	4¼" × 40"			
Muslin Solid and Assorted Prints[2] 1¼ (1) yds. each	16 (12)	2⅜" × 40"		72 (50)	B/C/B
	8 (6)	4¼" × 40"			

[1]Join strips lengthwise, alternating colors as shown.
[2]Print strips should be evenly distributed among mustard, blue, green, and brown prints.

FIRST CUT			SECOND CUT	
Fabric and Yardage	Number of Pieces	Size	Number of Pieces	Shape
PLAIN PATCHES				
Muslin Solid 3½ (2½) yds.	15 (10)	8" × 40"	71 (49)	D
SPEEDY TRIANGLE SQUARES *				
Muslin Solid and Med. Brown Print ¾ yd. each	2	19½" square	48 (40)	E/E
Muslin Solid and Dk. Brown Print ¾ yd. each	2	19½" square	52 (44)	E/E

*See *Speedy Triangle Squares*, page 95. Mark 4 × 4 grids with 4⅝" squares.

The size of this quilt can be adjusted easily from full/queen to twin by decreasing the number of center blocks to make 2 fewer rows and 2 fewer columns, and decreasing the number of border blocks accordingly. Refer to the cutting charts (page 37) for the number of pieces to cut for the different sizes.

FULL/QUEEN
71 plain center blocks and 72 pieced center blocks in an 11 × 13 layout; quilt center 82½″ × 97½″

TWIN
49 plain center blocks and 50 pieced center blocks in a 9 × 11 layout; quilt center 67½″ × 82½″

GREAT SIZING TIP

Because this pattern will repeat continuously no matter how many blocks are placed in each row or column, you can plan your quilt to be almost any size you wish. Just remember that the length of each edge will be a multiple of 7 ½″ (width of each block; also the width of a pair of border strips). Some examples:

5 blocks in a 5 × 1 layout = 15″ × 45″ table runner

9 blocks in a 3 × 3 layout = 30″-square wallhanging

48 blocks in a 6 × 8 layout = 45″ × 60″ crib quilt

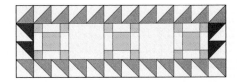

Pieced Center Block

Join units as shown to make one block. Make 72 blocks (full/queen) or 50 blocks (twin).

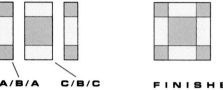

A/B/A   C/B/C

**FINISHED PIECED
CENTER BLOCK**

Quilt Center

Arrange blocks as shown, alternating plain and pieced blocks; make sure the prints/ colors are evenly distributed; refer to the photographs on pages 34 and 42 for color placement on our quilt. Join blocks to make rows. Join rows.

FULL/QUEEN

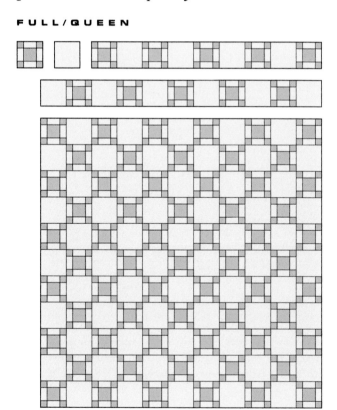

TWIN

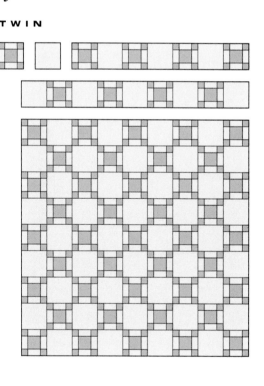

Border

Directions are given below for full/queen. Differing amounts for twin are given in parentheses. Refer to the Components diagram on page 35 for orientation of triangle squares on all sides of quilt. Note that the top and bottom strips are mirror images, as are left- and right-side strips. See the *Great Border Tip*, below, for alternate corner settings.

1. Join 24 (20) muslin/med. brown E/E's to make 2 short strips.
2. Join 26 (22) of muslin/dk. brown E/E's to make 2 long strips.
3. Join border to quilt center, first long strips at sides, then short strips at top and bottom.

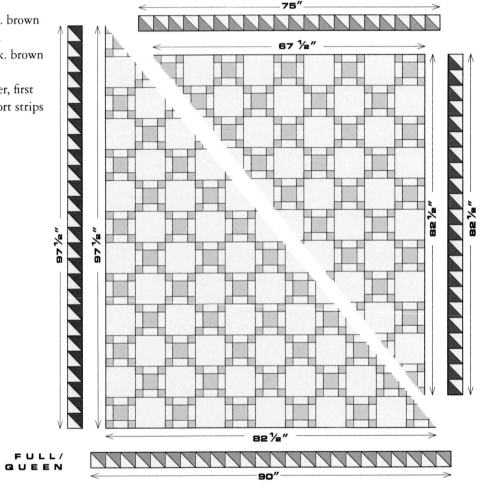

TWIN

75"

67 ½"

97 ½"

97 ½"

82 ½"

82 ½"

82 ½"

90"

FULL/ QUEEN

GREAT BORDER TIP

On this antique quilt, all of the triangle squares in each border strip have the same orientation, which creates four different border corners. You can change the orientation of the end triangle squares of the top and bottom border strips to change the corner patterns.

Finishing

1. Mark quilting designs on quilt top.
- *For pieced center blocks:* Mark an allover on-point square grid, using corners of patches as a guide.
- *For plain center blocks:* Connect centers of sides to mark a large on-point square. Continue marking pattern of small grid squares in corners of plain block, stopping at large square. Mark lines for inward echo quilting inside large square as shown.

- *For border blocks:* Mark lines for inward echo quilting on muslin solid triangle in each block as shown. Do not mark brown triangles.
2. Prepare batting and backing.
3. Assemble quilt layers.
4. Quilt on all marked lines.
5. Trim batting and backing even with quilt top.
6. Bind quilt edges.

GREAT ACCESSORY IDEA

You can make a 15"-square throw pillow, or a pair of them, from the components of the Puss in the Corner quilt. Frame a block with triangle squares, then assemble the layers and quilt them. Add a pillow back and stuff with fiberfill, or insert a 15"-square knife-edge pillow form.

 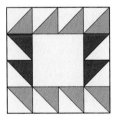

In this pattern, alternating pieced and plain blocks create a lattice; the fewer colors you use, the stronger the lattice will appear. Reversing or redistributing light and dark elements will alter the overall effect. Use a high-contrast palette for a traditional interpretation, or shade your hues subtly across the surface for one that is unique.

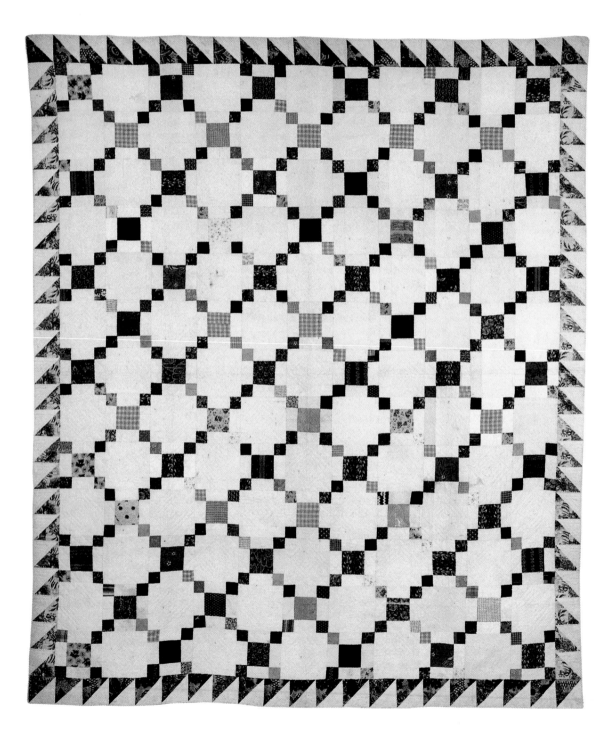

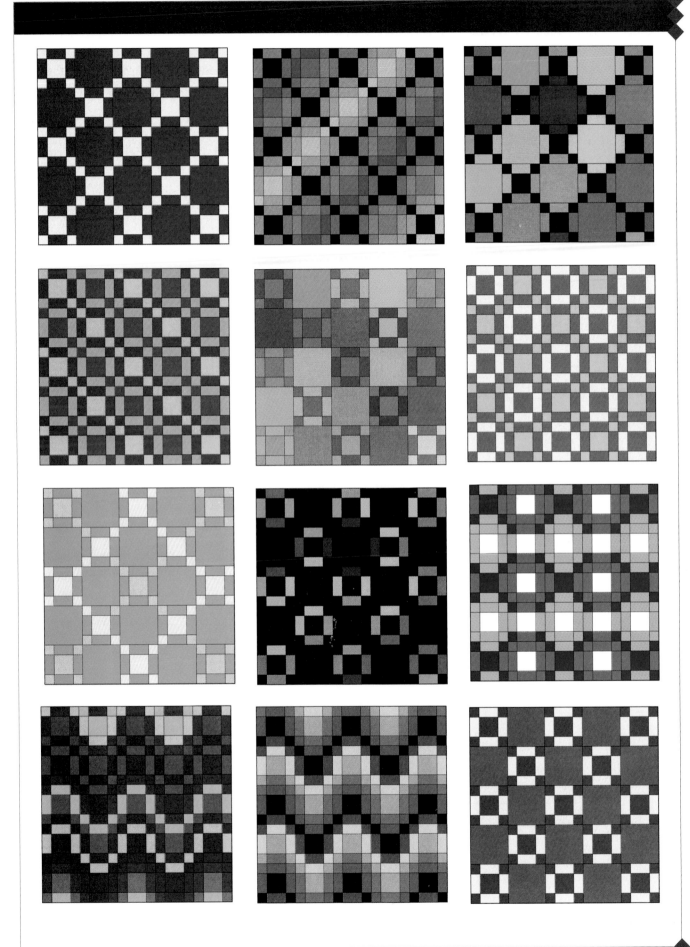

Photocopy this page, then create your own color scheme using colored pencils or markers. Refer to the examples shown, or design a unique arrangement to match your decor or please your fancy. Try using color to accent or define hidden patterns —heart, diamond, X, or zigzag.

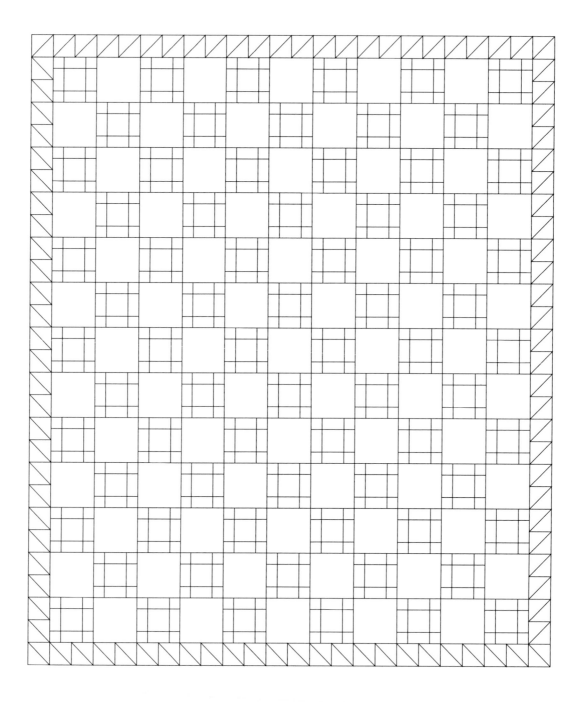

Y ou can create many classic quilts from the Puss in the Corner block. Vary the setting angle from straight to diagonal, add sashing, or omit the plain blocks and use positive/negative pieced blocks. Adding sashing or using a diagonal set will change the size of the quilt; use plain borders or recalculate the triangle squares.

Watercolor Gallery

BY FRANCES CALHOUN, JUDITH DOENIAS AND JEAN PERRY

Watercolor washes inspired these impressionistic quilts, in which patches of light and dark print fabrics shimmer into shapes and images. The book Watercolor Quilts, by Pat Maixner Magaret and Donna Ingram Slusser, has created a great interest in this fascinating technique. Here, by manipulating color values and print densities on a grid of squares, three quilters have painted wonderful pictures. Follow our directions to create your own interpretations.

If you are fascinated by the interplay of light and shadow, and if you are wondering how to utilize all of those wonderful print fabric scraps you have been accumulating, then turn your creativity to a watercolor quilt—no two will ever be identical.

Choose one of the designs offered here, or make a design of your own; see the *Great Planning Idea* on page 48. If you like, use markers to create the basic palette on your chosen plan. When you are satisfied with your design, select your fabrics: Look at the printed motifs and lines first, and then shift your focus to value and intensity. Choose colors both pure and dull; turn a square wrong side up to soften its effect.

 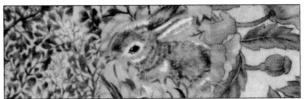

◆ Select medium- to large-scale prints such as florals, animals, fruits and vegetables, tropical, ethnic or holiday prints, and juvenile, sports, or hobby motifs.

◆ Choose asymmetrical and uneven prints; squares cut from different sections of these will look very different. Look also for fabrics that seem to suggest texture, mood, or motion, such as marble, water, or clouds.

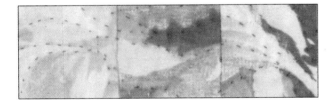 

◆ Include both monochromatic and multicolor prints. Choose similar multicolor prints that will appear to flow and merge seamlessly when placed next to each other.

You will need a large collection of precut fabric squares (be sure to include seam allowance). Many quilters find cutting 2″ squares very convenient, but you can use any size from 1½″ to 2½″; anything smaller would be difficult to handle, and anything larger would weaken the overall effect. Use a window template to see exactly how each print will look on the finished square.

Sorting Your Palette

Once you have a good selection of squares, you are ready to arrange your palette. A low, flat box such as from pizza or soda cans makes a handy sorting and storage tray. Sort the squares in rows, according to value. A typical palette might include nine rows:

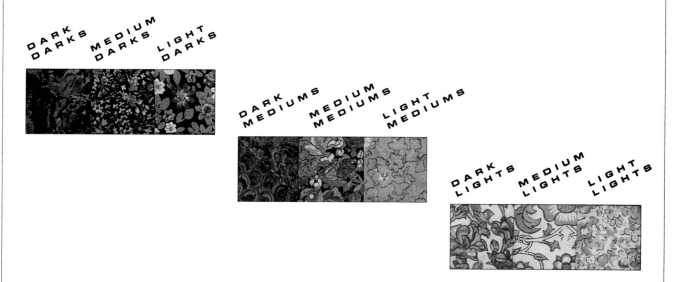

After the initial sorting, move a short distance away, squint your eyes at your palette, and see if any of the squares seem out of place. If your eye stops or is drawn to any individual square as you look along the row, move it to a more appropriate row.

GREAT PLANNING IDEA

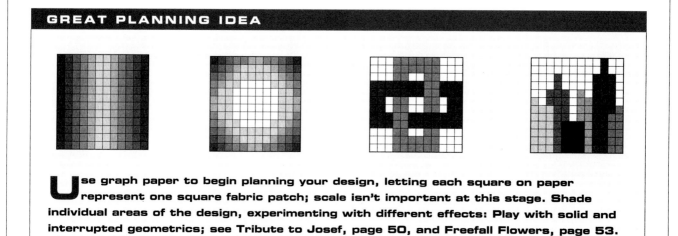

Use graph paper to begin planning your design, letting each square on paper represent one square fabric patch; scale isn't important at this stage. Shade individual areas of the design, experimenting with different effects: Play with solid and interrupted geometrics; see Tribute to Josef, page 50, and Freefall Flowers, page 53. Consider adding triangle squares where diagonal lines seem appropriate as on Reflection, page 51. Or try adding an appliqué as on Forest Clearing, page 52.

Arranging the Pieces

For the final step in designing your watercolor quilt, you will need a vertical surface such as a wall or large board covered with thin polyester batting or some other material to which your fabric squares will adhere without pinning and on which they can be easily moved around. Following your graph paper plan, begin to put paint to canvas: Arrange the squares on your design wall, focusing on getting the values in the right place. When the grid is complete and your design roughed out, then you can begin the detail work.

Here are some general guidelines you might consider for a successful design:

- ◆ Use only a few squares from any one fabric.
- ◆ Don't place squares from the same fabric near each other.
- ◆ Use only a few of the very lightest and/or very darkest squares.

Step back from the design wall at least 8 feet. Better yet, walk out of the room for a while, then come back and look at the wall with a fresh eye. To get a better idea of the relative values, you can squint at your design, look at it through a red plastic filter (which doesn't work too well on reds), the viewfinder of your camera, or a reducing glass. By doing this, the individual prints will disappear and you will see the overall effect more objectively. If a square looks out of place or seems to have the wrong lines or the wrong value, rotate or replace it.

Walk out of the room again, then come back later that day or the next, and continue making periodic adjustments until you are satisfied with your design.

Stitching the Pieces

Devise a plan for joining the pieces so that you will be able to keep them not only in order, but also in the proper orientation. After all the time spent on your layout, you don't want to lose your design by inadvertently rotating the pieces.

- ◆ Work with one row at a time, pinning the pieces together as you remove them from the wall.
- ◆ Once the row is stitched, place it back on the wall, with the correct edge toward the top.

If you put some thought into the assembly order, you may be able to plan a system by which to stack the pieces on your machine table and position and sew them on one by one, but pins will assure that they stay in the proper orientation.

Concentric and alternating light and dark squares are clearly delineated on this watercolor geometric.

In counterpoint to the straight set patches and motif squares, the wallhanging features an allover on-point square grid of quilting lines that cuts across the seams at the corners of individual patches and helps to camouflage them.

The quilt is framed by a separate, continuous binding with a finished width of 1/4″.

1 square = 1″

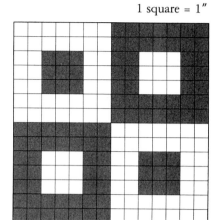

196 squares in a 14 × 14 layout

Judith Doenias made this small piece in remembrance of painter Josef Albers, whose work includes a series of paintings titled *Homage to the Square.*

Light, medium, and dark areas compose a landscape on this wallhanging. Most of the squares in the quilt center are plain patches, while the slopes of the mountain and its reflection are shaped by 26 pieced triangle squares.

Two borders frame the quilt center, one ½″ wide and one 3″ wide. The corner squares of the second border are pieced in triangular quarter-sections to create identical symmetrical designs.

Random horizontal swirls of quilting add a sense of motion both above and below the water line. To indicate air currents, swirls are spaced about 1½″ apart; as water currents, ¼″ to ¾″ apart.

The quilt has self-binding, with the quilt top and backing folded in and slipstitched together.

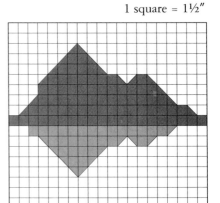

1 square = 1½″

360 squares in a 20 × 18 layout

Frances Calhoun's marvelous use of fabric captures the magic of changing and reflected light.

Corners of medium and dark foliage frame the light, sunny clearing at the center of this forest scene. The black silhouette of the standing buck is fused to the patchwork, eliminating the need for stitching slender legs and antlers; see the actual-size appliqué pattern on page 96.

The quilt has two borders, one ½″ wide and one 2½″ wide. Swirls of randomly spaced, quilted air currents enliven the design. A circular line of quilting representing the sun emanates rays of quilted sunlight downward to illuminate the clearing.

The quilt has self-binding, with the quilt top and backing folded in and slip-stitched together.

A dappled and nearly real scene by Frances Calhoun.

1 square = 1½″

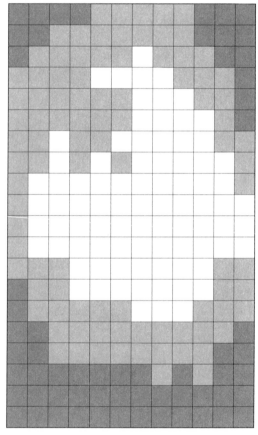

240 squares in a 12 × 20 layout

Medium-value flowers sprawl across this patchwork garden, occasionally interrupting the areas of dark and light that are a labyrinthine hedge and background.

A single flower in the top left seems about to float off the quilt, since its upper edge has been cut to match the outline of its floral print instead of the upper edge of the quilt. Swirls of quilted air currents waft across the scene in lines about ½″ apart.

The quilt has self-binding, with the quilt top and backing folded in and slip-stitched together.

1 square = 2″

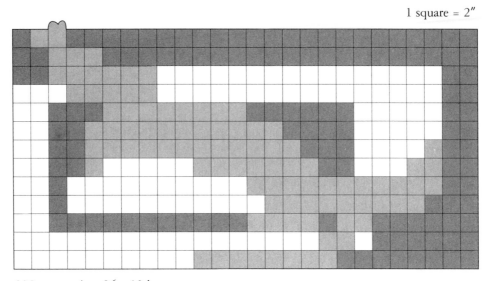

338 squares in a 26 × 13 layout

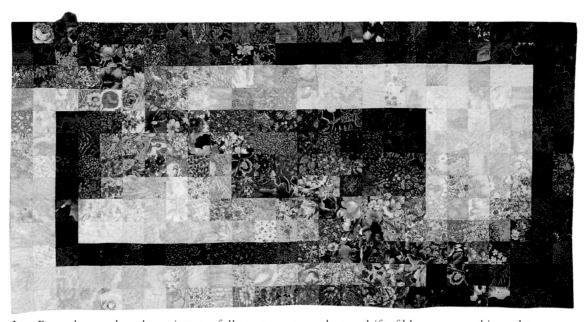

Jean Perry chose and cut her prints carefully to create an exuberant drift of blooms across this garden.

Geometry #1

BY CAROLE YVETTE LYLES

An urge to explore the ways in which ethnic prints could be combined led Carole Lyles to design this vibrant quilt. The bold prints are interspersed with black and mustard solids and set simply in pieced and plain horizontal bands. Carole's work often explores spiritual themes but in this piece the fabrics—African-inspired and American-made—reflect her African-American background. To make a similarly personal quilt, choose fabrics that are important to you and see their effect in this graphic pattern.

Note: All dimensions except for binding are finished size.

QUILT CENTER
Pieced center, 18″ × 25″

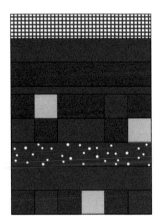

BINDING
1¼″-wide strip, pieced as
necessary and cut to size

FABRIC AND CUTTING LIST

Yardages are based on 44″ fabric. Prepare templates, if desired, referring to drafting schematics. Cut strips and patches following cutting schematics and chart; see *Using the Cutting Charts*, page 92. Cut binding as directed below. Except for drafting schematics, which give finished sizes, all dimensions include ¼″ seam allowance and strips include extra length, unless otherwise stated. (NOTE: Angles on all patches are 90°.)

DIMENSIONS

FINISHED QUILT
18″ × 25″

GREAT BINDING TIP

If you want to make bias binding, you will need an additional ¼ yd. of black solid. Cut strips on a 45° diagonal and piece as needed.

MATERIALS

MUSTARD SOLID
¼ yd.

YELLOW/ORANGE/ GREEN PRINT
¼ yd.

BLACK/WHITE CHECK
¼ yd.

BLACK/WHITE PRINT
¼ yd.

BLACK SOLID
¾ yd.

BINDING
Use ¼ yd. black solid, cut and pieced, to make a 1¼″ × 100″ straight-grain strip.

BACKING *
¾ yd.

BATTING *

THREAD

*Backing and batting should be cut and pieced as necessary so they are at least 4″ larger than quilt on all sides, then trimmed to size after quilting.

FIRST CUT			SECOND CUT*	
Fabric and Yardage	Number of Pieces	Size	Number of Pieces	Size/Shape
Mustard Solid ¼ yd.	1	3½″ × 15″	3	A
Yellow/Orange/ Green Print ¼ yd.	1	3½″ × 30″	7	A
	—	—	1	B
	—	—	1	3½″ × 18½″
Black/White Check ¼ yd.	—	—	1	3½″ × 18½″
Black/White Print ¼ yd.	—	—	1	3½″ × 18½″
Black Solid ½ yd.	1	3½″ × 20″	4	A
	—	—	1	B
	—	—	1	1½″ × 18½″
	1	3½″ × 40″	2	3½″ × 18½″

* Strips are exact length.

DRAFTING SCHEMATICS
(No seam allowance added)

CUTTING SCHEMATICS
(Seam allowance included)

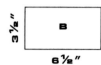

QUILT ASSEMBLY

Quilt Center

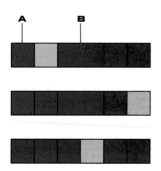

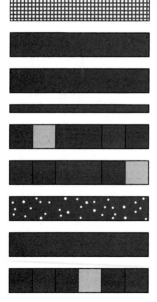

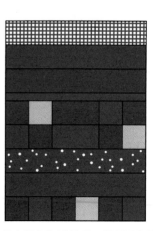

1. Assemble A and B patches as shown to make 3 pieced strips.

2. Arrange plain and pieced strips as shown. Join strips.

FINISHED QUILT CENTER

Finishing

1. Prepare batting and backing.
2. Assemble quilt layers.
3. Quilt in-the-ditch around black solid A's and B. Single-outline quilt around individual motifs on yellow/orange/green print as desired. Fill plain black solid strips with machine-stippled loops; see *Machine-Stippling*, page 95.

4. Trim batting and backing to ⅜" beyond outermost seam line.
5. Bind quilt edges.

The prints you use will have as much influence on the mood of this quilt as the palette, but here are a few color variations to trigger your thoughts. Photocopy and color the diagram to work out your design.

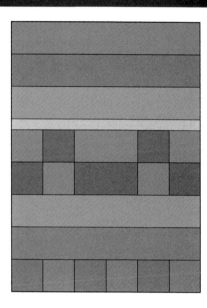

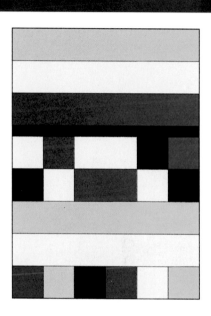

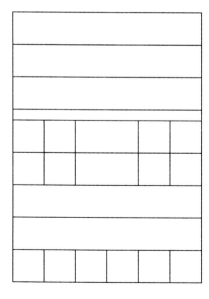

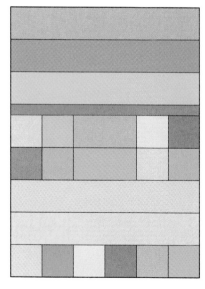

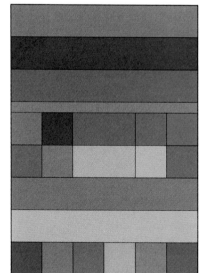

Bull's-Eye

BY JACQUELYN SMYTH

imple and strong, Bull's-Eye is one of the easiest patchwork patterns. All the border strips are the same width, all the corner squares the same size, and the piecing a snap. This graphic pattern also offers a good opportunity for the color-shy to experiment with palette; see pages 65 to 67. Jackie made the mini quilt as a swatch to test color and thought it so charming that she couldn't resist finishing it with a prairie point border; see page 62.

Note: All dimensions except for binding are finished size.

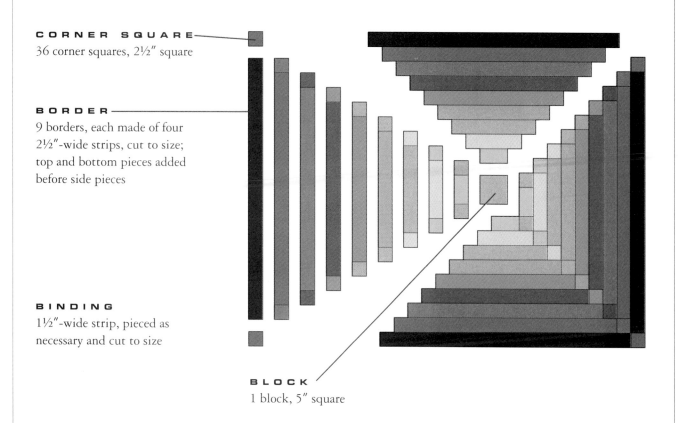

CORNER SQUARE
36 corner squares, 2½″ square

BORDER
9 borders, each made of four
2½″-wide strips, cut to size;
top and bottom pieces added
before side pieces

BINDING
1½″-wide strip, pieced as
necessary and cut to size

BLOCK
1 block, 5″ square

GREAT SIZING TIP

Because this pattern will repeat continuously no matter how many borders are placed around the quilt center, you can plan your quilt to be almost any size you wish; see the Great Border Tip, page 63, and the Great Changing the Shape Tip, page 64. Just remember that the length of each edge will be a multiple of 5″ (width of each center block; also the width of each pair of border strips). Some examples:

6 borders = 35″-square wallhanging

12 borders = 65″-square wallhanging

15 borders = 80″-square twin quilt

Yardages are based on 44″ fabric. Prepare templates, if desired, referring to drafting schematics. Cut strips and patches following cutting schematics and charts; see *Using the Cutting Charts*, page 92. Cut binding following cutting schematics, charts, and directions below. Except for drafting schematics, which give finished sizes, all dimensions include ¼″ seam allowance. Except for overall binding length, all strips are exact length. (NOTE: Angles on all patches are 90°.)

DIMENSIONS

FINISHED QUILT
50″ square

GREAT BINDING TIP

If you want to make straight-grain binding from a single print, you will need an additional ½ yd. of fabric.

To make a single-print bias binding, you will need ¾ yd. of fabric. Cut strips on a 45° diagonal and piece as needed.

MATERIALS

LT. MUSTARD PRINT
½ yd.

MED. MUSTARD PRINT
¾ yd.

DK. MUSTARD PRINT
¾ yd.

LT. GREEN PLAID
¼ yd.

MED. GREEN PRINT
½ yd.

DK. GREEN PRINT
1¼ yds.

LT. LAVENDER PRINT
¼ yd.

MED. VIOLET PRINT
½ yd.

DK. RED-VIOLET PRINT
1½ yds.

BINDING
Use remainder of fabric from first, fourth, and seventh borders, cut and pieced, to make a 1½″ × 210½″ straight-grain strip; see schematics and cutting chart.

BACKING *
3½ yds.

BATTING *

THREAD

*Backing and batting should be cut and pieced as necessary so they are at least 4″ larger than quilt on all sides, then trimmed to size after quilting.

FIRST CUT			SECOND CUT	
Fabric and Yardage	Number of Pieces	Size	Number of Pieces	Size/Shape
PLAIN PATCHES [1]				
Lt. Mustard Print[2] ½ yd.	—	—	4	B
	1	3″ × 40″	4	3″ × 5½″
Med. Mustard Print[2] ¾ yd.	—	—	4	B
	4	3″ × 20½″		
Dk. Mustard Print[2] ¾ yd.	—	—	4	B
	4	3″ × 35½″		
Lt. Green Plaid ¼ yd.	—	—	4	B
	2	3″ × 40″	4	3″ × 10½″
Med. Green Print ½ yd.	—	—	4	B
	4	3″ × 25½″		
Dk. Green Print 1¼ yds.	—	—	4	B
	4	3″ × 40½″		
Lt. Lavender Print ¼ yd.	—	—	1	A
	—	—	8	B
	2	3″ × 40″	4	3″ × 15½″
Med. Violet Print ½ yd.	—	—	4	B
	4	3″ × 30½″		
Dk. Red-Violet Print 1½ yds.	4	3″ × 45½″		

[1] Cut strips first, then cut squares from remainder of fabric.
[2] Reserve remainder of fabric for binding.

DRAFTING SCHEMATICS

(No seam allowance added)

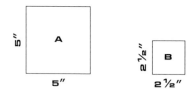

CUTTING SCHEMATICS

(Seam allowance included)

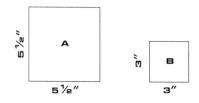

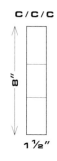

FIRST CUT			SECOND CUT		
Fabric and Yardage	Number of Pieces	Size	Method	Number of Pieces	Shape
STRIP-PIECED BINDING*					
Lt. Mustard Print, Med. Mustard Print, Dk. Mustard Print	2	3" × 40"		28	C/C/C
	2	3" × 40"			
	2	3" × 40"			

*Use remainder of fabric from borders and plain patches. Join strips lengthwise as shown.

GREAT DESIGN IDEA

You can make a mini quilt by reducing the size of the components in the full-size wallhanging. Cut the center block 2" square, and the border strips and corner squares 1¼"-wide.

Assemble the quilt top, then cut 24 light green squares, each 2⅝" square, to make prairie point edging with 6 points on each side as shown below; see Prairie Points, page 94.

Borders

Join borders to quilt center in sequential order (all sides of first border, then second border, etc.) as directed below.

1. Stitch corner squares to side strips.

2. Join each border to quilt center, first plain strips at top and bottom, then pieced strips at sides.

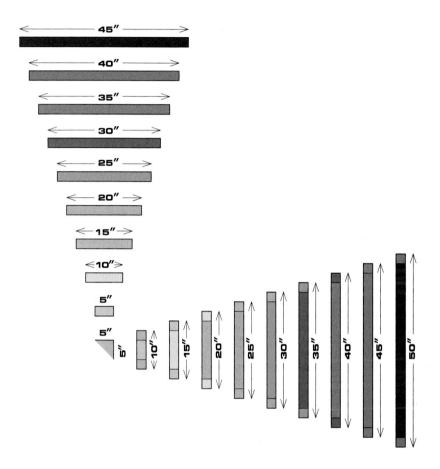

GREAT BORDER TIP

If you study the borders on the Bull's-Eye quilt, you will notice three distinct bands, each made of three consecutive borders. The bands generally progress in value from light to dark as your eye moves from the first band outward.

Each color (mustard, green, and purple) is used for one set of strips and one set of corner squares in each band, and the colors are in the same relative locations on all bands. Notice also that the color and value of the corner squares in each border are the same as those of the strips in the previous border, which results in light corner squares in the medium-value band and medium squares in the dark-value band.

To maintain the integrity of the pattern when changing the size of your quilt, increase or decrease the number of borders in groups of three (one complete band). If you are increasing the number of bands, plan your quilt so that the bands darken from the center outward; see also Changing Colors on page 65 for other arrangements.

Finishing

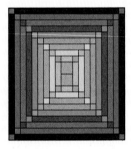

1. Mark quilting designs on quilt top.
- *For square patches:* Mark diagonal lines connecting pairs of opposite corners.
2. Prepare batting and backing.
3. Assemble quilt layers.
4. Quilt in-the-ditch on all seams. Quilt on all marked lines.

5. Trim batting and backing to ½" beyond outermost seam line.
6. Prepare binding.
- *For three-print binding:* Join C/C/C units to make a 1½" × 210½" strip (extra length included).
7. Bind quilt edges.

GREAT CHANGING THE SHAPE TIP

You can design a rectangular version of the Bull's-Eye quilt by changing the shape of the quilt center. Add one or more blocks to the center to make a row, then frame them with borders cut to size. You can also add more borders to enlarge the quilt further; see the Great Border Tip, page 63. Just remember that the length of each edge will be a multiple of 5" (width of each center block; also the width of each pair of border strips).

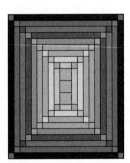 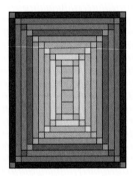 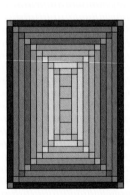

Palette and color arrangement both influence the overall effect of this pattern. You can choose a monochromatic, analogous, or high contrast scheme. You can also change the way the colors are placed or repeated to emphasize concentric bands, quadrants, or the X made by the corner squares.

Photocopy this page, then create your own color scheme using colored pencils or markers. Refer to the examples shown, or design a unique color scheme to match your decor or please your fancy.

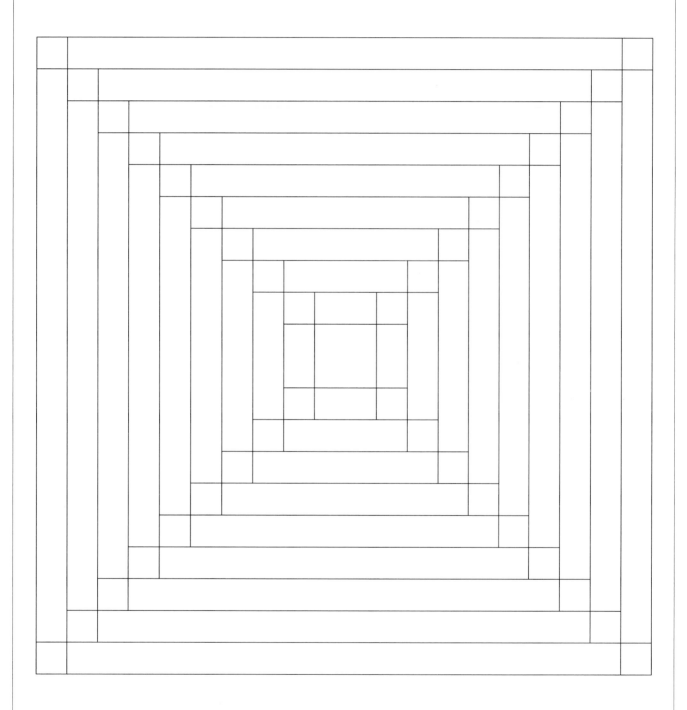

Trip Around the World

There are indeed a lot of squares in this antique quilt, but don't stop to count them—strip-piecing takes the tedium (and most of the individual patches) out of the pattern. We've broken the overall patchwork into manageable blocks, which, despite the apparent diagonal grid, are straight set. You do need to pay careful attention to the illustrations, and stitch with precise seam allowances, but this quilt is not nearly as tricky as it looks. The fabric used here is cotton sateen in solid colors.

Note: All dimensions except for binding are finished size. This quilt is a nonstandard size. It may be big enough for a double bed if you turn it sideways—use the length of the quilt across the width of the bed. Refer to Adjusting the Size, *page 73, and the* Great Sizing Tip, *page 74, to enlarge the quilt by adding a border.*

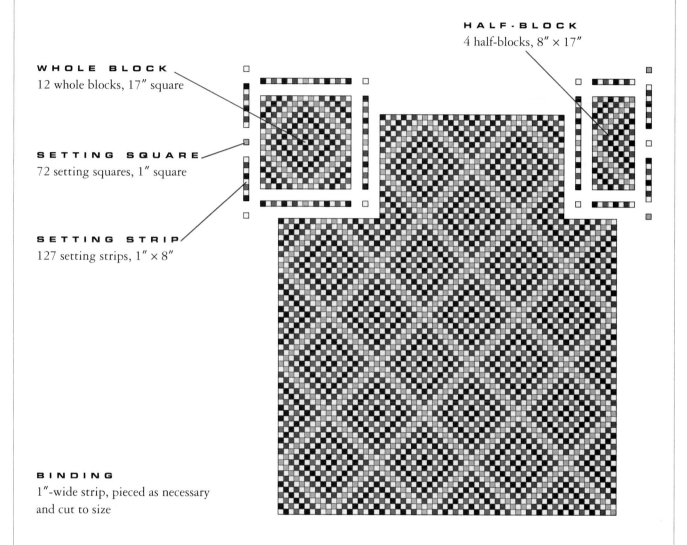

HALF-BLOCK
4 half-blocks, 8″ × 17″

WHOLE BLOCK
12 whole blocks, 17″ square

SETTING SQUARE
72 setting squares, 1″ square

SETTING STRIP
127 setting strips, 1″ × 8″

BINDING
1″-wide strip, pieced as necessary
and cut to size

GREAT ACCESSORY IDEA

You can make a 19″ throw pillow to match the Trip Around the World quilt. Frame a whole block with one row of setting strips to make a 19″-square (finished size) pillow top. Layer the pillow top, batting, and backing, then quilt in-the-ditch on all seams. Add a pillow back and trim such as piping or a ruffle, if you wish, and stuff the pillow firmly with fiberfill.

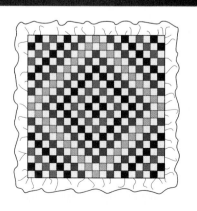

Note: Differing sizes and amounts for full/queen are given in parentheses.

Yardages are based on 44″ fabric. Prepare templates, if desired, referring to drafting schematics. Cut strips and patches following schematics and charts; see *Using the Cutting Charts*, page 92. Cut binding as directed below. Except for drafting schematics, which give finished sizes, all dimensions include ¼″ seam allowance and strips include extra length, unless otherwise stated. (NOTE: Angles on all patches are 90°.)

DIMENSIONS

FINISHED WHOLE BLOCK
17″ square

FINISHED HALF-BLOCK
8″ × 17″

FINISHED QUILT
64″ × 73″ (82″ × 91″)

GREAT BINDING TIP

If you want to make bias binding, you will need an additional ½ yd. of brick solid. Cut strips on a 45° diagonal and piece as needed.

MATERIALS

☐ **ECRU SOLID**
5¼ (8¼) yds.

▨ **MUSTARD SOLID**
1¼ (4½) yds.

■ **BRICK SOLID**
1¾ (4¾) yds.

■ **SLATE SOLID**
½ (3¼) yds.

■ **OLIVE SOLID**
2 (5) yds.

BINDING
Use ½ yd. brick solid, cut and pieced, to make a 1″ × 300″ (1″ × 370″) straight-grain strip.

BACKING *
5 (8) yds.

BATTING *

THREAD

*Backing and batting should be cut and pieced as necessary so they are at least 4″ larger than quilt on all sides, then trimmed to size after quilting.

DRAFTING SCHEMATICS
(No seam allowance added)

SQUARE

1″ · 1″

CUTTING SCHEMATICS
(Seam allowance included)

SQUARE

1½″ · 1½″

PIECED STRIP

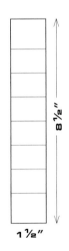

8½″ · 1½″

FIRST CUT			SECOND CUT		
Fabric and Yardage	Number of Pieces	Size	Method	Number of Pieces	Strip[1]
STRIP-PIECED PATCHES[2]					
Ecru Solid 1 yd.; Mustard, Brick, Slate and Olive Solids ¼ yd. each	20	1½″ × 40″	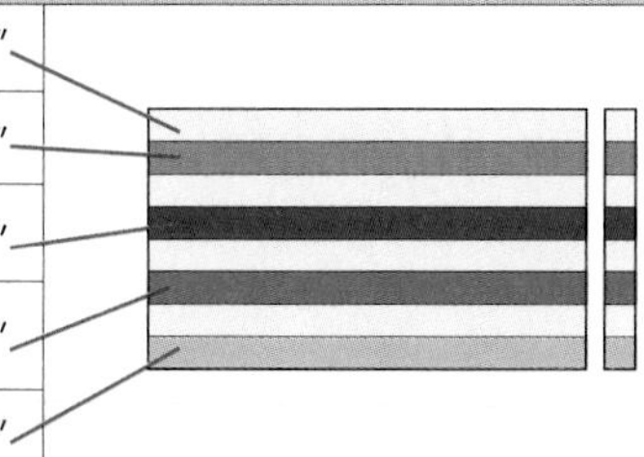	112	#1 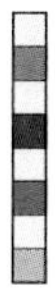
	5	1½″ × 40″			
	5	1½″ × 40″			
	5	1½″ × 40″			
	5	1½″ × 40″			
Ecru Solid 1 yd.; Mustard, Brick, Slate and Olive Solids ¼ yd. each	5	1½″ × 40″	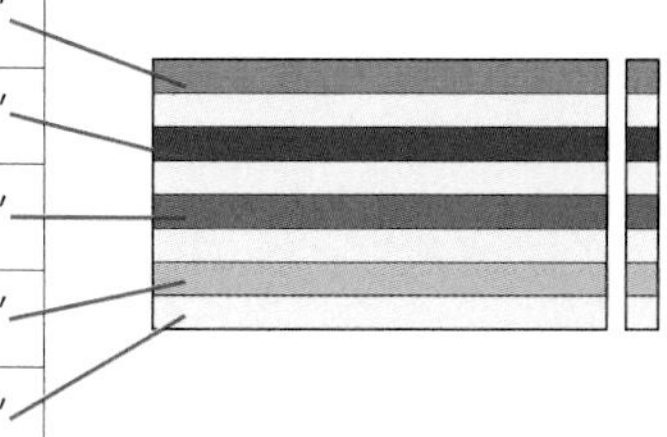	112	#2 
	5	1½″ × 40″			
	5	1½″ × 40″			
	5	1½″ × 40″			
	20	1½″ × 40″			
Ecru Solid 1 yd.; Olive Solid ½ yd.; Mustard and Brick Solids ¼ yd. each	20	1½″ × 40″	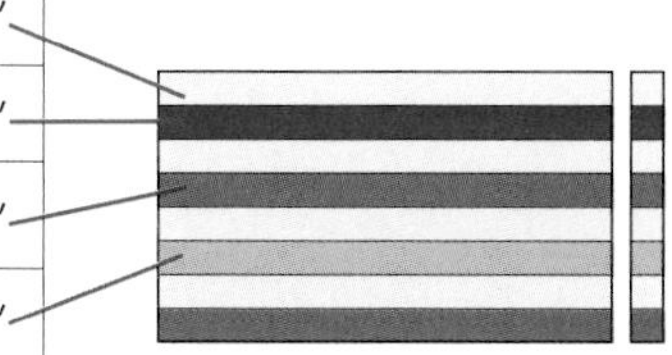	112	#3 
	5	1½″ × 40″			
	10	1½″ × 40″			
	5	1½″ × 40″			
Ecru Solid 1 yd.; Olive Solid ½ yd.; Mustard and Brick Solids ¼ yd. each	5	1½″ × 40″	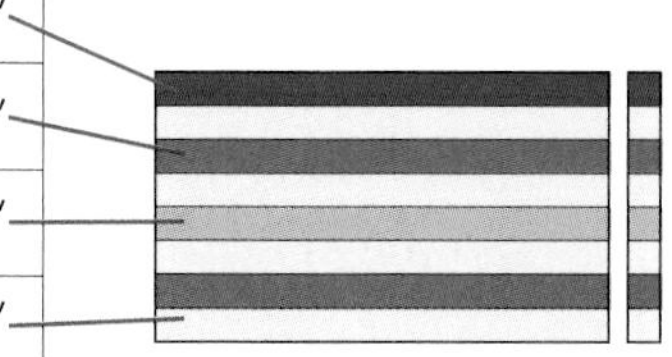	112	#4 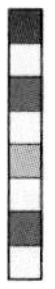
	10	1½″ × 40″			
	5	1½″ × 40″			
	20	1½″ × 40″			
Ecru Solid 1 yd.; Brick Solid ½ yd.; Slate and Olive Solids ¼ yd. each	20	1½″ × 40″	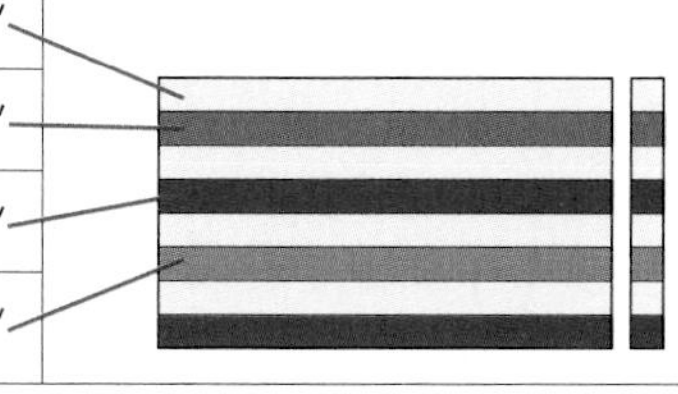	127	#5 
	5	1½″ × 40″			
	10	1½″ × 40″			
	5	1½″ × 40″			

[1] Strip #5 is for setting strips.

[2] Join strips lengthwise to make bands, alternating ecru with other colors as shown.

GREAT CUTTING TIP

All of the strips for the quilt center are the same size. Following is the total number to cut from each color:

Ecru: 102   Slate: 15
Mustard: 22   Olive: 35
Brick: 30

FIRST CUT			SECOND CUT	
Fabric and Yardage	Number of Pieces	Size	Number of Pieces	Shape
PLAIN PATCHES*				
Ecru Solid ¼ yd.	2	1½″ × 40″	36	Square □
Mustard Solid ¼ yd.	2	1½″ × 40″	36	Square ▩

*For full/queen, use remainder of fabric from border.

BORDER (FOR FULL/QUEEN)		
Fabric and Yardage	Number of Pieces	Size
Ecru Solid* 3 yds.	8	1½″ × 90″
	8	1½″ × 100″
Mustard Solid* 3 yds.	2	1½″ × 90″
	2	1½″ × 100″
Brick Solid 3 yds.	4	1½″ × 90″
	4	1½″ × 100″
Slate Solid 3 yds.	2	1½″ × 90″
	2	1½″ × 100″
Olive Solid 3 yds.	2	1½″ × 90″
	2	1½″ × 100″

* Reserve remainder of fabric for cutting plain patches.

GREAT DESIGN IDEA

You can reduce the time spent cutting and piecing a project based on the Trip Around the World quilt by enlarging the patches, which may reduce the number of patches needed. With enough enlarging, one whole block framed with setting strips might even be big enough to be a quilt in itself. Some examples:

2″ squares: 1 whole block with setting strips = 38″-square wallhanging

4″ squares: 1 whole block with setting strips = 76″-square twin coverlet

5″ squares: 1 whole block with setting strips = 95″-square full/queen coverlet

The size of this quilt can be adjusted easily from twin to full/queen by adding a border. Refer to the cutting chart, opposite, and the *Great Sizing Tip*, page 74.

TWIN
64″ × 73″; 12 blocks,
4 half-blocks, no border

FULL/QUEEN
82″ × 91″; 12 blocks,
4 half-blocks, one 9″-wide
pieced border

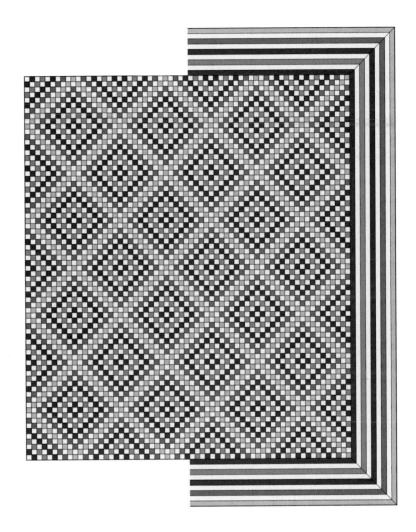

GREAT DESIGN TIP

If you find the components of the Trip Around the World quilt confusing, omit the half-blocks and work with whole blocks and setting strips only. Because the pattern will repeat continuously no matter how many blocks are placed in each row or column, you can plan your quilt to be almost any size you wish. Just remember that the length of each edge will be a multiple of 18″ (one block and one setting strip) plus 1″ (one setting strip to balance the pattern). Some examples:

6 whole blocks in a 2 × 3 layout = 37″ × 55″ crib quilt

20 whole blocks in a 4 × 5 layout = 73″ × 91″ twin quilt

30 whole blocks in a 5 × 6 layout = 91″ × 109″ full/queen quilt

I f you want to make a 96" × 105" full/queen quilt rather than the 82" × 91" coverlet we give directions for, you can enlarge your project by simply widening the border, as shown below.

Instead of using nine 1"-wide strips for each border side, use 17 strips, cutting them 1" × 106" and 1" × 115". Join the border to the quilt and finish it as usual.

Whole Block

Directions are given below for making one whole block. Amounts for making all 12 whole blocks at the same time are given in parentheses.

1. Arrange strips as shown. Join strips to make 8 (96) eighth-blocks.

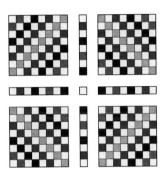 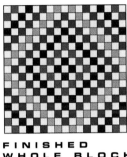

2. Join eighth-blocks in pairs, rotating one as shown, to make 4 (48) quarter-blocks.

3. Arrange quarter-blocks, setting strips, and an ecru setting square, rotating strips and quarter-blocks as shown. Join units to make 3 rows. Join rows to make one (12) whole block.

FINISHED WHOLE BLOCK

Half-Block

Directions are given below for making one half-block. Amounts for making all 4 half-blocks at the same time are given in parentheses.

1. Make 2 (8) quarter-blocks in same manner as for whole block, Steps 1 and 2.

2. Join units as shown to make one (4) half-block.

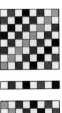 

FINISHED HALF-BLOCK

Quilt Center

1. Join 2 setting strips and a mustard square to make 31 long strips with red ends.

2. Join 2 setting strips and an ecru square to make 4 long strips with ecru ends.

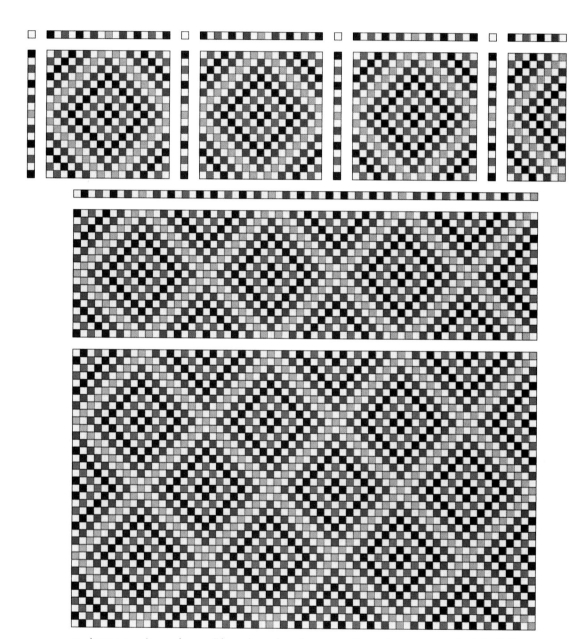

3. Arrange units as shown: Place the red-ended strips above, below, or to the left of the blocks and half-blocks; place the ecru-ended strips to the right of the half-blocks. Join units to make rows. Join rows.

Border (for Full/Queen)

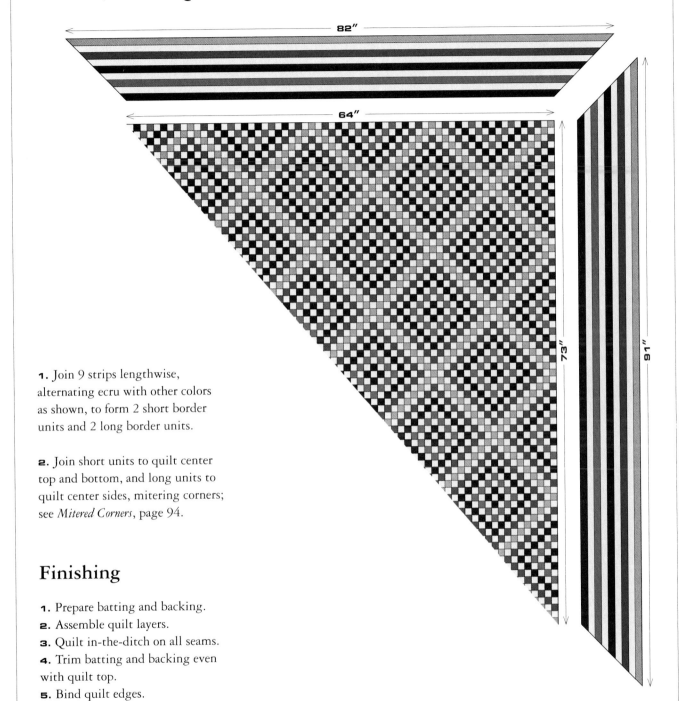

1. Join 9 strips lengthwise, alternating ecru with other colors as shown, to form 2 short border units and 2 long border units.

2. Join short units to quilt center top and bottom, and long units to quilt center sides, mitering corners; see *Mitered Corners*, page 94.

Finishing

1. Prepare batting and backing.
2. Assemble quilt layers.
3. Quilt in-the-ditch on all seams.
4. Trim batting and backing even with quilt top.
5. Bind quilt edges.

The repeated block used in this interpretation of the Trip Around the World pattern establishes a strong diagonal lattice on an ecru ground. Replace the ecru patches with black for more drama, with soft mustard for subtlety. For a sweeter look, replace each of the colors with a pastel. Use prints to soften the overall effect. Note that the colored illustrations on the following pages each show one block without the sashing strips that complete the lattice.

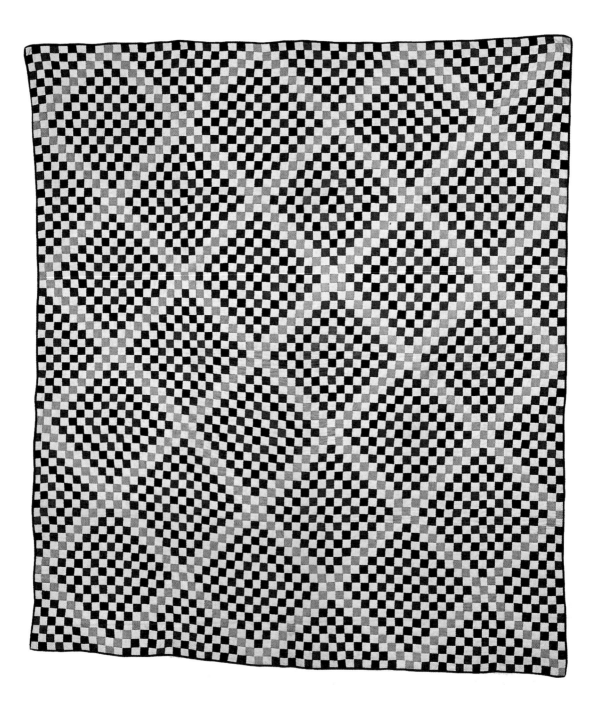

Photocopy this page, then create your own color scheme using colored pencils or markers. To retain your sanity, be sure to maintain the concentric alternation of colors within the block, as shown on the preceding pages. For our strip-piecing directions to work, you must make a color-for-color substitution.

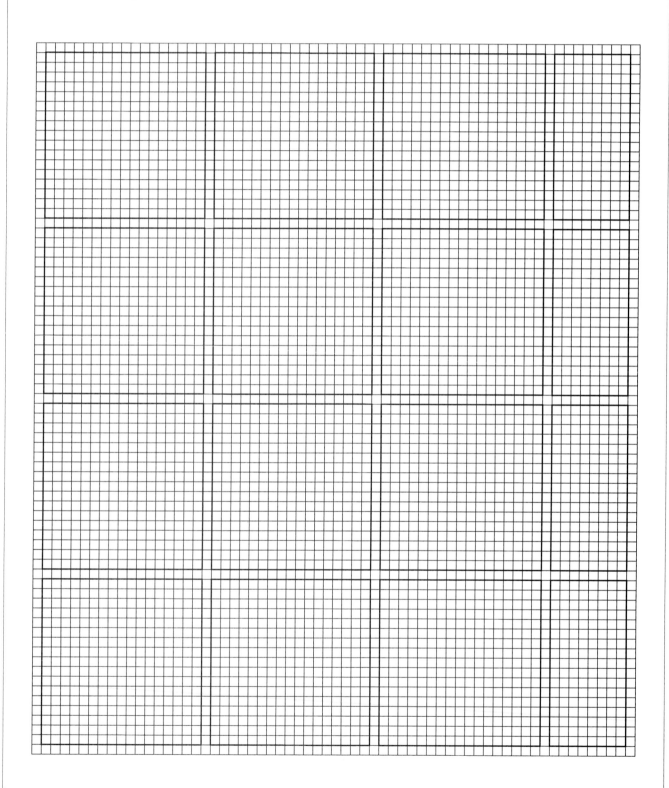

I f you have the confidence to refigure our piecing directions, you can vary the Trip Around the World color scheme in other ways. Add more colors, or shade them subtly from dark to light. You can even make the area inside the lattice different from the corners of the block to create an overall checkerboard effect.

Chevron

BY DIANE RODE SCHNECK

Diane Schneck shared an old quilt top from her collection with us, saying, "I know this seems really straightforward, but I've never been able to figure out the logic behind its assembly." At first glance, the perpendicularly butted rectangles seem a Log Cabin variation, but a closer look shows there is no way to assemble this pattern without sewing a considerable number of inside corners. Diane accepted the challenge to find a logical way to make this small mat; turn to page 88 to see the antique that was its inspiration.

Note: All dimensions except for binding are finished size.
We have selected a representative color to depict the assorted light, medium, and
dark blue prints of the quilt center. Refer to the photographs, opposite and on page 89,
to see the actual colors and their distribution.

BLOCK
One block, 11¾″ square

FIRST BORDER
Four strips, two ¾″ × 11¾″
and two ¾″ × 13¼″; side pieces
added before top and bottom pieces

SECOND BORDER
Four strips, two 1⅝″ × 13¼″ and
two 1⅝″ × 16½″; side pieces added
before top and bottom pieces

BINDING
1½″-wide strip, pieced as necessary
and cut to size

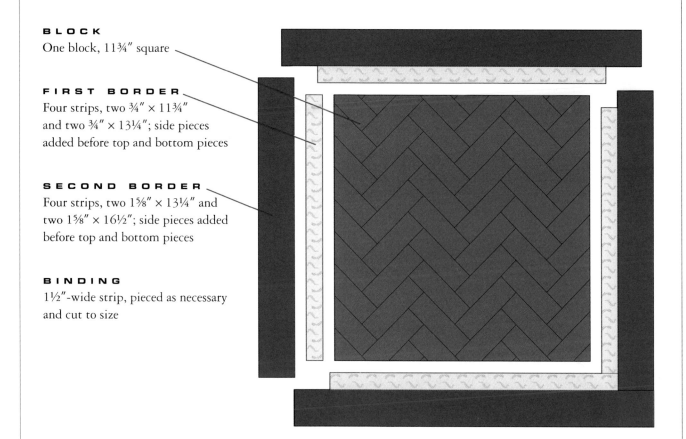

FABRIC AND CUTTING LIST

Yardages are based on 44″ fabric. Prepare template, if desired, referring to drafting schematic. Cut strips and patches following cutting schematic and chart; see *Using the Cutting Charts*, page 92. Cut binding as directed below. Except for drafting schematic, which gives finished size, all dimensions include ¼″ seam allowance and strips include extra length, unless otherwise stated. (NOTE: Angles on all patches are 90°.)

DIMENSIONS

FINISHED BLOCK
11¾″ square

FINISHED QUILT
16½″ square

DRAFTING SCHEMATIC

(No seam allowance added)

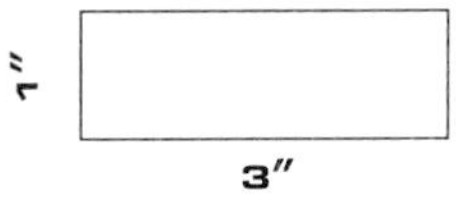

CUTTING SCHEMATIC

(Seam allowance included)

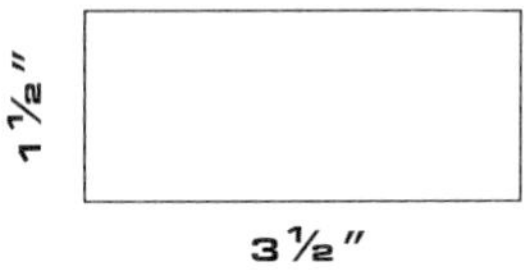

MATERIALS

LT. BLUE-ON-ECRU PRINT
½ yd.

ASSORTED BLUE PRINTS
Small amounts of at least 20 different lt., med., and dk. blue prints to total about ½ yd.

DK. BLUE PRINT
¾ yd.

BINDING
Use remainder of fabric from first border, cut and pieced, to make a 1½″ × 80″ straight-grain strip.

BACKING*
¾ yd.

BATTING*

THREAD

*Backing and batting should be cut and pieced as necessary so they are at least 4″ larger than quilt on all sides, then trimmed to size after quilting.

Fabric and Yardage	Number of Pieces	Size/Shape
PATCHES[1]		
Assorted Blue Prints ½ yd.	66	Rectangle
FIRST BORDER[2]		
Lt. Blue-on-Ecru Print ½ yd.	2	1¼″ × 12¼″
	2	1¼″ × 13¾″
SECOND BORDER[3]		
Dk. Blue Print ¾ yd.	2	2⅛″ × 13¾″
	2	2⅛″ × 17″

[1] Cut an equal number of rectangles from each print.
[2] Strips are exact length. Reserve remainder of fabric for binding.
[3] Strips are exact length.

GREAT BINDING TIP

If you want to make bias binding, you will need an additional ¼ yd. of lt. blue-on-ecru print. Cut strips on a 45° diagonal and piece as needed.

Block

Assemble block as directed; see the *Great Piecing Tip*, below, and the photographs on pages 82 and 89 for actual colors of rectangles and their distribution.

1. Stitch 2 rectangles together.

2. Stitch a rectangle to bottom left side of piece from Step 1.

3. Stitch a rectangle to bottom right side of piece from Step 2.

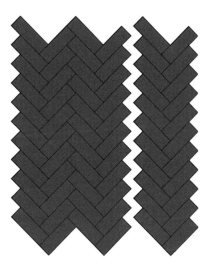

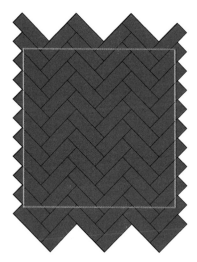

4. Continue adding rectangles to make a 2 × 11 column. Make 3 columns.

5. Arrange columns as shown. Join columns; see the *Great Assembly Tip*, page 86.

6. Mark a centered 11¾″ square on assembled block. Stay-stitch just outside the marked line (seam line). Trim away excess fabric outside seam line, leaving ¼″ seam allowance.

FINISHED BLOCK

GREAT PIECING TIP

Use a window template or transparent ruler as a guide to mark stitching lines on all rectangles. All seam lines should be marked before stitching.

Mark, press, and handle your project carefully (and as little as possible) until the first border is added, to prevent the bias edges of the block from stretching before they are stitched to the straight-grain edges of the border. Do not slide the iron; lift and replace it.

Stitching the seam that joins two columns of chevrons involves sewing many inside corners; it is important to stitch exactly on the seam lines and not into the seam allowance. To assemble the quilt you will be stitching a series of short seams along the zigzag edges of the columns, which you might find easier to do by hand than by machine; secure the ends of each seam with backstitching.

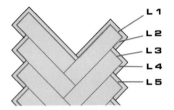

L1
L2
L3
L4
L5

R1
R2
R3
R4
R5

LEFT COLUMN

RIGHT COLUMN

1. Place left chevron column over right column as shown, aligning seam lines L1 and R1. Stitch L1/R1; finger press.

2. With left column still on top, align seam lines L2 and R2, rotating layers as shown. Stitch L2/R2; finger press.

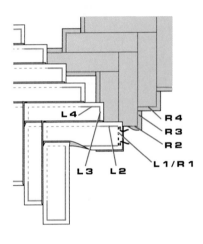

L4
L3   L2
L1/R1
R4
R3
R2

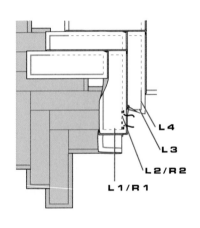

L4
L3
L2/R2
L1/R1

3. Continue stitching seam lines in sequential order.

4. Press the seam allowance after each short seam is stitched or wait until each zigzag seam has been stitched along its entire length. Press seam allowances as shown.

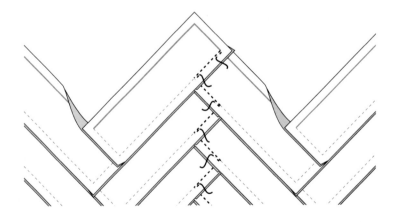

Borders

Join borders to quilt, first short strips at sides, then long strips at top and bottom. Complete first border before proceeding to second.

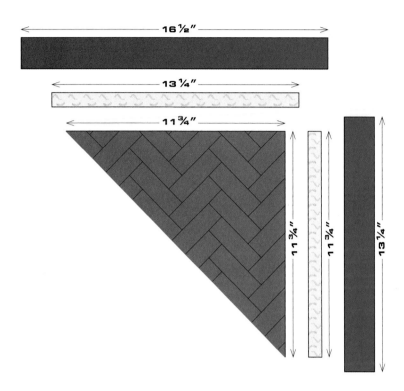

Finishing

1. Mark quilting designs on quilt top.

♦ *For second border:* Use a transparent ruler or template to mark an unbroken line of 1″ -wide on-point squares so that there are 16 squares on each border side.

2. Prepare batting and backing.

3. Assemble quilt layers.

4. Quilt in-the-ditch on inner and outer border seams, and along zigzag seams connecting 1 × 11 halves of each 2 × 11 column. Quilt on all marked lines.

5. Trim batting and backing to ½″ beyond outermost seam line.

6. Bind quilt edges.

You can plan a Chevron block to be almost any size by changing the size and/or number of the components.

- ◆ The rectangular patches can be enlarged to almost any size, but should be reduced to no smaller than ½"; changing the height/width ratio of the rectangle's sides will also alter the appearance of the chevrons.
- ◆ To lengthen your project, add more pairs of rectangles to each column. To widen it, add more columns.
- ◆ Note that it is also possible to join columns of different-sized chevrons. Cut all the rectangles from strips of the same width, but make the length different for one or more columns. The longer the rectangles are in proportion to their width, the wider the column will be.

On this 84" × 94" antique quilt top, the rectangles are 1¾" × 6¼" and there are nine 2 × 36 columns.

This pattern is sometimes known as Coarse Woven, and it is filled with zigzags and columns; the way you place color in it will change its appearance as much as the palette you use. Whether you work in jewel tones or pastels, prints, stripes, or solids, consider using a contrasting element to trace a path over your quilt's surface.

Photocopy this page, then create your own color scheme using colored pencils or markers. Refer to the examples shown, or design a unique color scheme to match your decor or please your fancy. If you choose a monochromatic palette, use a variety of prints, as Diane did, or the pattern will disappear.

Appendix

The sample cutting charts and schematics below demonstrate how these elements work together to provide the information needed to cut most of the pieces for any quilt project in the Better Homes and Gardens® Creative Quilting Collection volumes. Any additional cuts, such as for binding, can be found in the Fabric and Cutting List for each project.

DRAFTING SCHEMATIC

Drafting schematics, which do not include seam allowance, are provided for your convenience as an aid in preparing templates.

DRAFTING SCHEMATIC
(No seam allowance added)

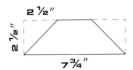

CUTTING SCHEMATIC

Cutting schematics, which do include seam allowance, can be used for preparing templates (with seam allowance included) but are given primarily as an aid for speed-cutting shapes using a rotary cutter and special rulers with angles marked on them.

CUTTING SCHEMATICS
(Seam allowance included)

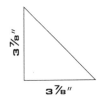 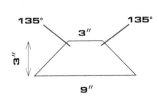

FABRIC AND YARDAGE

This column gives the color and amount of fabric needed to cut groups of shapes, rounded up to the next ¼ yard. To change the color scheme of a project, refer to the dimensions given for individual groups of shapes and use (combine them as needed) to calculate the new yardage.

FIRST CUT

Cut the number of pieces in the sizes indicated on either the lengthwise or crosswise grain unless otherwise stated, using templates or rotary cutting rulers. For 40″-long strips, cutting completely across the width of the fabric usually provides the most economical cuts.

SECOND CUT

Cut the number of pieces in the sizes and/or shapes indicated, referring to the cutting schematics for angles and cut sizes. Reversed pieces are designated by a subscript $_R$ (e.g., the reverse of a B patch is designated B_R) and can frequently be obtained from the same strips as their mirror images by cutting the two shapes alternately.

BORDER

From ½ yd. blue check cut two 2½″ × 29″ and two 2½″ × 32″ border strips.

FOOTNOTE

Use the cited instructions for Speedy Triangle Squares and mark the grids in the layout indicated.

APPLIQUÉS

From ¼ yd. red floral cut 16 flowers and 8 buds. From ¼ yd. blue floral cut 56 leaves. Reversed pieces are designated by a subscript $_R$ and these patterns should be turned over before marking onto fabric.

FIRST CUT			SECOND CUT	
Fabric and Yardage	Number of Pieces	Size	Number of Pieces	Shape
PLAIN PATCHES				
Red Solid ¼ yd.	1	3⅞″ × 20″	8	A
	1	3½″ × 40″	8	B
White Solid ¼ yd.	1	3⅞″ × 20″	8	A
	1	3½″ × 40″	6	C
SPEEDY TRIANGLE SQUARES				
Red Solid and White Solid ½ yd. each	2	16½″ × 20⅝″	72	B/B
BORDER				
Blue Check ½ yd.	2	2½″ × 29″		
	2	2½″ × 32″		

[1]See *Speedy Triangle Squares* (page 00). Mark 4 × 5 grids with 3⅞″ squares.

8 RED SOLID A'S

From ¼ yd. red solid, cut one 3⅞″ × 20″ strip. From strip cut four 3⅞″ squares. Cut squares in half to make 8 right-triangle A's.

6 WHITE SOLID C'S

From ¼ yd. white solid cut one 3½″ × 40″ strip. From strip cut six trapezoids.

FOOTNOTE REFERENCE

See the footnote underneath the chart for additional information about cutting this group of shapes.

APPLIQUÉS		
Fabric and Yardage	Number of Pieces	Shape
Red Floral ¼ yd.	16	Flower
	8	Bud
Blue Floral ¼ yd.	56	Leaf

Refer as well to Great Quiltmaking: All the Basics, *the detailed companion to the volumes in the* Better Homes and Gardens® Creative Quilting Collection.

Mitered Corners

Mitered corner seams are stitched by hand or by machine, as directed below, after all the border strips have been machine-stitched to the quilt center. For multiple borders, the strips for an individual quilt edge are joined together to form a strip set, which is then treated as a single border strip.

HAND-STITCHED MITER

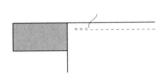

1. Stitch each border strip to quilt, beginning and ending ¼" from quilt ends; secure with back-stitching.

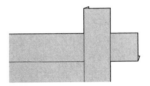

2. Place quilt flat, right side up, lapping border strip ends.

3. At one corner, press under the upper strip end on a 45° angle. Slipstitch folded edge to strip underneath. Press. Trim excess fabric.

MACHINE-STITCHED MITER

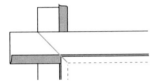

1. Stitch border strips to quilt in same manner as for hand-stitched miter, Step 1. Place quilt flat, wrong side up, lapping border strip ends.

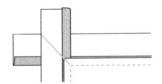

2. At one corner, mark a 45° diagonal on the upper strip end. Reverse lapping to mark underneath strip.

3. Fold quilt corner on the diagonal, right sides together, with edges even and seam allowances pressed away from border. Align and pin together marked lines on border strips. Stitch on one marked line, beginning at inner border corner. Press. Trim excess fabric.

Prairie Points

1. Press fabric squares in half diagonally twice, right side out (see individual project directions for size and amounts).

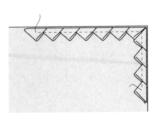

2. Pin triangles evenly along edges of project front with all double-folds facing the same direction. Lap adjacent edges, or slip single-folds inside double-folds. Stitch on seam line.

Speedy Triangle Squares

1. Cut matching pieces of two contrasting fabrics (see individual project directions for dimensions).

2. Mark a square grid on wrong side of lighter-color fabric, leaving ½″ margin all around grid. Mark half as many grid squares as triangle squares needed; each marked square will make two pieced squares. (NOTE: Mark grid squares ⅞″ larger than desired finished size of triangle squares.)

3. Mark diagonals across squares.

4. Pin marked fabric to contrasting fabric, right sides together. Stitch ¼″ from each diagonal, on both sides of line.

5. Cut along marked lines, grid lines first and then diagonals.

6. Remove corner stitches.

7. Open triangles. Press seams toward darker fabric.

Machine-Stippling

Always make a sample to test the effect of the stippling on the fabric and batting in your project: Your quilting lines should look smooth and even on both the front and back; adjust the tension on the threads in the machine as necessary.

Place your quilt in a hoop (one that will fit easily under your sewing machine needle) to keep the layers smooth and taut. Reposition the hoop during quilting as necessary.

Use a darning or embroidery foot, and either lower or cover the feed dogs so that you have complete control over the movement of the quilt through the machine. There is no need to adjust the stitch length. Control the needle speed with the motor-control pedal as usual, and guide the fabric in the desired pattern with your hands.

Forest Clearing
(page 52)

ACTUAL-SIZE PATTERN

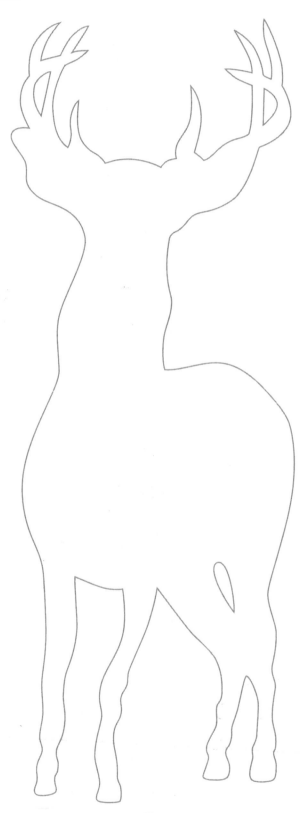